W9-BUI-802

DATE DUE

GAYLORD			PRINTED IN U.S.A.

The Four Seasons
of Success

W HEN HERMAN MELVILLE *died in 1891, the literary journal of the day,* The Critic, *did not even know who he was.* . . .

The older generation remembered that Herman Melville had once been famous. He had adventured in the South Seas on a whaler; he had lived among the cannibals; and in Typee *and* Omoo *he had made a romantic pastiche of his experiences. On these books Mr. Melville's fame had been founded: it was a pity he had not done more in this line; for his later books, obscure books, crowded books that could be called neither fiction nor poetry nor philosophy nor downright useful information, forfeited the interest of a public that liked to take its pleasures methodically.* . . . *Both the fame and the later absence of recognition, Mr. Melville's commentators agreed, were deserved. By his interest in* . . . *metaphysics, Mr. Melville carried his readers into a realm much too remote, and an air too rarefied; a flirtation with South Sea maiden, warm, brown, palpable, was one thing: but the shark that glides white through the sulphurous sea was quite another. In* Moby-Dick, *so criticism went, Melville had become obscure: and this literary failure condemned him to personal obscurity.* . . .

—FROM LEWIS MUMFORD'S PREFACE TO *Herman Melville* (1929)

BY BUDD SCHULBERG

What Makes Sammy Run?
The Harder They Fall
The Disenchanted
Waterfront
Some Faces in the Crowd
Across the Everglades (Screenplay, with introduction)
A Face in the Crowd
   (Screenplay, with introduction by Elia Kazan)
The Disenchanted (Play, with Harvey Breit)
What Makes Sammy Run?
   (Musical, libretto with Stuart Schulberg)
From The Ashes—Voices of Watts
   (edited, with an introduction)
Sanctuary V
Loser and Still Champion: Muhammad Ali
The Four Seasons of Success

✧✧ BUDD SCHULBERG

The Four Seasons of Success

✧
✧
✧
✧

DOUBLEDAY & COMPANY, INC.
GARDEN CITY, NEW YORK
1972

Some of this material has been previously published in periodicals: *Esquire*, "Saroyan: Ease and Unease on the Flying Trapeze," "Taps at Reveille," "Lewis: Big Wind from Sauk Centre," "Old Scott: The Mask, the Myth and the Man," Copyright © 1960 by Esquire, Inc.; *Newsday*, material on John Steinbeck, Copyright © 1969 by Newsday, Inc., reprinted by permission.

ISBN: 0-385-00510-5
LIBRARY OF CONGRESS CATALOG CARD NUMBER: 72-76202
COPYRIGHT © 1972 BY BUDD SCHULBERG
ALL RIGHTS RESERVED
PRINTED IN THE UNITED STATES OF AMERICA
FIRST EDITION

TO THE MEMORY OF SAXE COMMINS—
an editor for all seasons—
who nursed three Nobel Prize winners
and a brace of Pulitzer Prizers
through bountiful summers and bitter winters

Contents

*The Four Seasons
of Success*

Introduction

IN PRECEDING CENTURIES and carrying over into our breakaway twentieth, it was par for the literary course for writers to know each other. There were circles like the Lambs', to which the established authors of their day, Carlyle, Coleridge, De Quincy, and other peers would naturally gravitate to gossip, complain, and exchange ideas with Charles and Mary on their Friday Afternoons. If novelists were not personal friends involved with each other like Melville and Hawthorne, they were at least professional acquaintances like James and Wells. Diametrically opposed in style and outlook, the latter pair considered it one of their literary duties to express their differences in an urbanely combative correspondence.

Before the First World War it was still common for literary folks to fraternize. There was Mabel Dodge's salon for movers and shakers in Greenwich Village, where John Reed, Edna St. Vincent Millay, Big Bill Heywood, and other artists and actionaries passing through would assemble for poetry reading, wine drinking, lovemaking, and revolutionary dreaming. There was the Chicago School of Carl Sandburg, Edgar Lee Masters, Sherwood Anderson, along with a marqueeful of only slightly lesser lights—Ben Hecht, Charles MacArthur, Louis Weitzenkorn—drinking, praising, and damning together. Even in the Jazz Age it was still literary etiquette for a young man of promise to send politely autographed copies of his new book to Edith Wharton, T. S. Eliot, or other established literary figures of his day. There was every sort of exchange, from Scott Fitzgerald's genteel tea-time encouragement from Edith Wharton and Eliot, to his Long Island drinking bouts with Ring Lardner. There were stormy confrontations: Hemingway vs. Max Eastman, chest to chest in their editor's office; Hemingway vs.

Morley Callaghan with an embattled Fitzgerald holding a controversial stopwatch on their boxing match in a Paris gymnasium; Fitzgerald vs. Thomas Wolfe in an exchange of literary positions more acrimonious than Wells' and James'.

When most of our good young writers of the twenties stayed on in Paris after the war or migrated there to escape what professional grump H. L. Mencken called the American "booboisie," they found literary camaraderie and enemy groupings at Gertie Stein's and at the clubby bookshop of Sylvia Beach: not only Fitzgerald, Hemingway, and Lewis dedicated themselves to congenial expatriatism, but also Kay Boyle, Robert McAlmon, Ramon Guthrie, Archibald MacLeish, Henry Miller, Carl Van Vechten, and the mad rich poet Harry Crosby, who lived in a celebrated windmill with his fabulous Caresse.

Back home in those days when *Life* was a humor magazine and the President of the United States was someone to chuckle over rather than demonstrate against, the Hotel Algonquin regulars included wits who could float like butterflies and sting like bees: Dorothy Parker, Heywood Broun, George S. Kaufman, Robert Benchley, Alexander Woollcott, and others just as mean and merry. Eventually that caustic Camelot fell apart as a score of the best writers in New York went West to make a lot of money writing dialogue for the talkies. One day I stood in the Garden of Allah in Hollywood, by Alla Nazimova's enormous swimming pool that was said to have been built according to the siren's whim in the shape of the Black Sea, on which she had lived in her Crimean childhood. The exotic pool was surrounded by pseudo-exotic stucco villas shaded by banana trees, loquats, and other tropical growth. I had just stepped out of the bungalow rented year after year by Edwin Justus Mayer, once a distinguished New York playwright (*Children of Darkness, The Firebrand*), with whom I was collaborating on an undistinguished Bob Hope comedy for Sam Goldwyn. I heard the unmistakable laughter of Bob Benchley, one of the nation's pre-eminent humorists, then the property of Metro-Goldwyn-Mayer. I remember looking around in wonder at those bogus villas where some of America's better writers clustered together for warmth: in those back-lot Spanish beds slumbered or tossed Donald Ogden Stewart, S. J. Perelman, John O'Hara, Corey Ford, Scott Fitzgerald—some of them, like Scott, Benchley, and Eddie Mayer, seemingly trapped in the Garden of Allah like flies to honey paper, others merely passing through, like Marc Connelly, Woollcott, and Lillian Hellman. But what a gathering of literati it was, at Benchley's never-closing bar, with Dorothy Parker, Samuel Hoffenstein, Somerset Maugham, and a rare assortment of the more literate drinking actors, Bogart and Barrymore, Errol Flynn, Charlie Butterworth, and the Laughtons. It was almost as if the Algonquin Round Table had been moved cross country into the Garden and under the palm trees. Only the banter was underlined with more bitterness here as so many of the writers knew they were debasing themselves and did their clever best to laugh off their shame in pointed jokes about their studio bosses.

Those days of literary affinity have long since been fractured and fragmented. Even the boys in the back room of the good old Stanley Rose Book Store on Hollywood Boulevard, where we used to drink orange wine and talk Life and Literature with Bill Saroyan, Pep (Nathanael) West, John Fante, Horace McCoy, Aben Kandel, Jo Pagano, and other young hopefuls, no longer have a back room to go back to, or the energy or wish to establish another.

No, those were groupier days. And the spirit of *now* seems to be summed up in the porcupine manifesto of a standoffish writer I pass occasionally in the night: "I don't want to meet other writers." The last literary group to hang together were probably those wandering beatifics, Jack Kerouac, Allen Ginsberg, William Burroughs, Gregory Corso, John Clellon Holmes, Lawrence Ferlinghetti, and the other beloved infidels who expressed their contempt for the straight life of the Eisenhower days by taking to the road and becoming "generation outlaws" with a passion and a vengeance.

Today a William Styron acknowledges a John Updike at a

thinking man's cocktail party on Martha's Vineyard, and James Jones and Irwin Shaw may occasionally join together to relive the literary café life in Paris that Hemingway and his friends and rivals put so much of themselves into nearly half a century earlier. When Vance Bourjaily comes to Mexico he may call on me because we are fellow-novelists who like to go pre-Columbian temple-crawling together. When I come to San Francisco I call on Barnaby Conrad and we get together with Herbert Gold, Herb Caen, and other convivial literary types in that convivially literary city. Norman Mailer is a catalyst and thinks of himself with some justice as a latter-day Papa Hemingway, and he has his male and female groupies, including writers he occasionally likes to hit or who would like to hit him. But his would be described more accurately as a coterie than a writing circle. New York City has its oases for night-birds and if you drop into Elaine's you will probably find Jack Alexander, Bruce Jay Friedman, George Plimpton, and some other regulars, or down at the Lion's Head in the Village you can bump into fine two-fisted drinkers expressing social outrage at the bar—Pete Hamill and Joe Flaherty, Fred Exley, the poet Joel Oppenheimer. Mailer and Breslin are apt to breeze in and you will meet other convivial dissenters whose work you may happen to admire or enjoy putting down.

But ten years ago in a symposium on Writing in America, Alfred Kazin called ours "the Alone Generation," and although the currents of culture and counterculture in the early seventies would modify this description, there would seem to be more casual socializing than serious fraternizing. By the latter, one means the kind of circle Victor Hugo enjoyed, when such names as Alfred de Vigny, Madame de Staël, Dumas, de Musset, Balzac, Mérimée, Sainte-Beuve, Delacroix, Boulanger, Lamartine, Gautier, Goncourt, and others were not merely acquaintances rubbing shoulders at parties. They saw themselves as a group of romantic rebels, reacting against the common enemy and interreacting in a positive and creative way upon each other.

If I seem particularly interested in literary-group interreaction as well as in the spectacular and cruel stock market with its bulls and bears inflating and depressing authors' reputations, I came by it honestly, or at least early. As the son of a Hollywood studio head—an off-horse in that he was the only tycoon I ever met who preferred books to synopses and read Dickens, Melville, Conrad, Dostoevski, for pleasure—I was exposed at a tender age to the fierce and contrary winds of fortune, winds that seem to blow harder in America than anywhere else on earth. Ours is sometimes called the Great American Dream Machine but it may more properly be called the Great American Wind Machine. To create storm effects for motion pictures, technicians used a caged propeller, or wind machine, that would turn the stream from a water hose into a howling gale. When the director cried "Cut," the grip flipped a switch and the wind was silenced.

Great careers, attracting critical acclaim, a worshipful audience of millions throughout the world, and surrealistic salaries like ten thousand dollars a week, were turned on and off like wind machines. Close to home was the rise and fall of George Bancroft, a name that tips today's recognition scale like a weightless ghost. But in his day (late twenties—early thirties), Bancroft was King. When my father starred him in a Ben Hecht story directed by Josef von Sternberg, *Underworld,* Bancroft was rated the Number One box-office attraction in America. When we traveled to England with him, British reporters rushed aboard the *Ile de France* eager to know his answers to all the great questions of the day. Two blocks from the Tower of London our limousine was so completely surrounded by Bancroft-lovers that a special brigade of bobbies was needed to clear the way. At the entrance to the Tower he was mobbed by autograph hounds crying "G'o'ge, G'o'ge, shake m' hand, G'o'ge!" There were similar outbursts of Bancroft-hysterics in Paris, Berlin, and Vienna.

George Bancroft had been signed to one of those seven-year contracts that began at a lowly one thousand a week, with annual raises until the seventh year escalated to seventy-five hundred a week. When it came time for Bancroft's seventh-year high, my father called him into the throne room to give him the bad news. Bancroft was still a star, still a marquee name, but no longer the superstar he had been after *Underworld*. *Docks of New York* and *Thunderbolt* had done well but Jimmy Cagney and Paul Muni were beginning to replace George Bancroft as the world's favorite gangster. If he did not believe this slippage, my father told him, George could look at the account books himself. Paramount still wanted Bancroft on its roster (along with its new stars, Gary Cooper, Marlene Dietrich, Fredric March, Sylvia Sydney), but only if he would continue at his last established salary, six thousand a week. Three-hundred and twenty thousand dollars a year, in the days before taxes.

Bancroft was indignant. Bancroft was insulted. The studio, in the star-glazed eyes of George Bancroft, was lucky to have him at any price. Bancroft stalked out and waited for the rival studios to meet his price. Waited, all that year. And the next. And the next. There were offers at six thousand, then five thousand, and four thousand. But George Bancroft had been Number One and Number Ones must get their seventy-five hundred a week.

A few years later George Bancroft came back to work for my father in a film starring Edward Arnold (who was playing Bancroft-type roles now). And poor George was grateful for his three-hundred and fifty dollars a week.

Today, if you mention the name of the man who stopped traffic in all the capitals of Europe and whose infectious laughter was recognized and imitated all over the world, the kids who line up around the block for *The Godfather* and *The French Connection* will say, "George *who?* Bancroft? He was as big as Gene Hackman, huh? Man, you must be putting me on. I mean, I'm a film buff. I've seen Errol Flynn and Alan Ladd on the idiot box. But George *Bancroft* . . . ?"

And thus also, in my memory, did John Gilbert flash like a

falling star. From the world's great lover, on screen and off, with Greta Garbo, the Number One romantic lead between Valentino and Clark Gable, he plunged from world fame to the darkness of the unemployable. Up there in his castle in the hills of Beverly, in the classic style of the Hollywood romances, like Barrymore and Flynn and Ladd, he bitterly drank himself to death.

Ah, you may say, but what has Hollywood's sudden fame and fleeting fortune got to do with the real world, with the rest of the nation, and, most of all, with literature? Well, I have always believed that Hollywood is just like the rest of America, only more so. In other words, all the values of American society, the good ones and the false ones, are to be found in Hollywood, not realistically reflected but grotesquely magnified. Hollywood —or at least the overblown dream-factory town in which I was raised, the Hollywood of Monroe Stahr and the last tycoons— was like one of those distortion mirrors in amusement parks where a child is transformed into a giant, and a forefinger becomes the Tower of Pisa.

If I overlap the triumph and despair of the John Gilberts and the George Bancrofts with the migration of literary figures to Hollywood, it is because the innovation, the impact, of talking pictures that destroyed the Number Ones of the Silent Era brought to Hollywood a new wave of playwrights, novelists, poets, and critics. When my father, and other Hollywood moguls, saw that the "came-the-dawn" subtitle writers of the silent screen would not be able to write film plays for the Ruth Chattertons, the Fredric Marches, and the Barrymores, they threw a net over Broadway. The literary catch was pulled in and deposited on the Hollywood beach. Westward came Herman Mankiewicz, one of the wittiest lancers of the Algonquin Round Table, who had been drama critic of the *New York World* and *The New Yorker* and a playwright-collaborator of George S. Kaufman; Vincent Lawrence, the only man ever to have three plays running on Broadway at one time, and whom New York critics had favored as the writer most likely to write "the Great American Play"; John V. A. Weaver, in some ways a counterpart of Fitzgerald, contributor to the *Smart Set,* film critic for *Vanity Fair* and author of *In American* and other ground-breaking books of poetry in the twenties; Samuel Hoffenstein, a master of light verse (*Poems in Praise of Practically Nothing*); Eddie Mayer, mentioned earlier, a man of elegant talent and taste; Joseph Moncure March, author of the free-verse novels, *The Wild Party* and *The Set-Up*. The list is long and distinguished and sad. For I was to learn that they were greatly talented but troubled men. Each in his own way a cousin of Fitzgerald, gifted and doomed.

Each lot had more authors in residence than Oxford or Harvard. In one studio commissary you could break bread with Aldous Huxley, William Faulkner, Christopher Isherwood, Ben Hecht, Somerset Maugham, John Van Druten, Dalton Trumbo, Robert Sherwood—I pluck these stars at random from a darkening sky of nostalgia. There were the escapees, of course, those who cut their way through the invisible barbed wire and struggled back to their original line of work. Faulkner would manage to get back to Mississippi as soon as he had sobered up and collected his money. Isherwood seemed able to settle down and actually *write* in Santa Monica, and so did Huxley. Hollywood wasn't exactly Death Valley with every writer crawling to his death on the hot sand in search of gold like Frank Norris's *McTeague*. Still my youth was haunted by failed success. Dorothy Parker simply wasn't the short story phenomenon she had been ten years earlier. A piece would trickle into *The New Yorker* now and then, and there were plays written in collaboration that never quite lived up to the glittering reputation.

Why? Why so soon? Scott Fitzgerald had said, with eyes turned inward, "There are no second acts in American lives." There was Dottie Parker, with the same fine eye, the same impeccable ear, the same Wilkinson's blade of a mind, stewing in old juices, with talents rusting and falling into disuse—a touching complex of diminishing hopes, vicious wit, Victorian wiles, and a self-pity full of Scotch and rue. And all around her were friends and colleagues in a similar predicament. It seemed to me, as I walked through the Garden of Allah, that everybody I knew was a shooting star that had described its brilliant arc in the sky, lighting up its world for a moment in time, and then had burned out. Gifted and tormented people dreaming of that second act, a second chance: Herman Mankiewicz, who did write *Citizen Kane,* but mostly wasted his wit on mediocrity while determined to come back to the New York theater with *that play*. Vincent Lawrence, a love-scene specialist for drooping melodramas, who could positively recite *The Great Gatsby,* who could give Scott Fitzgerald lessons in writing dramatic dialogue, was forever resolving to shake the dream factory once and for all and restore himself to Eastern favor. He also had *that play* as his reentry permit to the world of the theater he had abandoned halfway through the first act of his life. And Eddie Mayer, whose dramas had been acclaimed for their literate theatricality in the twenties, and who had a genius for theater as prodigious as Dorothy Parker's for short story and light verse, lived with the tormented hope of returning to New York with a richly imaginative play called *Sunrise in My Pocket*.

Like poor lightning bugs in a bottle were "Mank" and "Dottie" and "Eddie" and the rest of that gifted tribe. All called great in their time and now nearly all forgotten, they had sunrise in their pockets but could not bring it forth to drive away the darkness. While it is usually assumed that Scott Fitzgerald is the ill-fated author dragged through the Winter Carnival in *The Disenchanted,* he had a distinguished predecessor. Several years earlier it had been John V. A. Weaver whom I, as an undergraduate, had invited to Dartmouth to address our literary society. And it had been the celebrated poet of the *Smart Set,* now turned film writer, who had fallen dead drunk into my callow arms as I waited to receive him at the White River Junction depot. Whether to deliver him in that state to the sedate Sanborn House of the Dartmouth College English Department or stay down in White River and join him in philosophical oblivion was my problem that day as it was to be, in a bizarre repetition, with Scott five years later. How a young admirer copes with a literary lion fallen into middle-aged despair is a crisis that has been resolved, like all such terrors, by the benevolent god of time. But the memory of the hurt, the repeated hurt, lives on in the form of a question. Why so soon? So soon for Parker, or lesser-known Mankiewicz? So soon for Fitzgerald, or lesser-known Weaver?

Oh, you say, that's too easy. Anyone can build a thesis on the basis of carefully selected weak sisters. And surely those who sacrifice the best years of their writing lives to the Hollywood assembly line and then weep over their fate are the weakest of sisters. All right, to extend our thesis, let us move out from Hollywood to a brother who made a fetish of strength, who abjured Hollywood, used it as a pejorative adjective, hailed artistic freedom and independence, and somehow confused it with the related institutions of South and North America, masochism and Number One-ism. We mean Papa. Big Hem. Proclaimed and self-proclaimed heavyweight champion of the world. *Now,* nobody is denying that Ernest Hemingway is the logical extension of Mark Twain and Stephen Crane and Frank Norris and Jack London and Sherwood Anderson and Gertrude Stein, to name some good ones who helped to hone the American language. Nobody is denying that those Hemingway up-in-Michigan stories, and a bookful of others, *live.* Nobody is denying that every writer and every reader, whether or not he Hems, is a better person, enriched, henceforth changed, by those stories, by that writing, the pure-as-a-pebble-tossed-into-an-unruffled-pond kind of writing, the writing that distinguishes even the novels marred by feminine sentimentality like *A Farewell to Arms,* but writing that proved that Mark and Frank and Jack and Sherwood knew what the obscenity they were writing about. Knew where they were going. Where *all* of them were going.

Now we come to the sickness. Not the lack of wonder that makes the best of Hemingway's work live, but the sickness, the American sickness (replace a few letters and you spell it success) that blew out his irreplaceable brains. He used the American language as a tight-coiled spring, he was a master of existentialism long before that word sprang into our vocabulary, as a nature writer he was the equal of Vance Bourjaily (high praise), and he had a deeper need than Vance for being loved, which was Hem's tough luck. And he had one other fantastic and outrageous American habit—he was a pioneer. Now, as we have suggested, he was no more a pioneer in the wilderness of the American language than Twain or Crane or Norris or Anderson—indeed a shade less of an innovator because he was further innovating their innovations. No matter, we love him like Daniel Boone. But there couldn't have been a Boone without a hundred Boones; that's both sociology and flat-out truth. However, the great American pioneer not only puts one foot in front of the other and pushes forward, he covers up the ground behind him in the brave conceit that no one has ever been there before and no one will be able to follow. You begin to see what is great and sick about America and why Papa Hemingway is so great and so sick? The great Papa would never truly acknowledge his debt to Mark or Steve or Sherwood or the rest of them. In fact he wrote a snotty little novel (*The Torrents of Spring*), taking off Sherwood Anderson just to prove how foolish was his model and how dead. Now, with the ground swept clean of the bones of the ancestors, Papa is ready to come forward as the inventor of the American language. You see how American he was, how marvelous, how full of crap, how creative, how sad, how "original," how self-destructive? It is bad enough when the critics call someone "Number One." One season it may be William Styron, another John Updike. They seem to need their "Number Ones." But when the writer thinks of himself as "Number One," not as a good mountain range of a writer, but as "Number One," like Texas in football, U.C.L.A. in basketball, and Johnny Carson on the midnight rube-tube, then that big number is in big trouble, competing not with his inner self but with his outer rating. Clearly, there was a moment in the career of Ernest Hemingway when the private spirit (a unique and highly sensitized one) gave way to the public image, a redundant and coarsened one. He who shunned Hollywood became more ravenous for publicity than Errol Flynn. In fact, they both had mustaches, they both did their work well, they both courted handsome women, and it became increasingly difficult to tell them apart. It was as if Gary Cooper were underplaying Hemingway on the screen while Hemingway was overplaying Errol Flynn in real life. Which, of course, he had, as we say, no business doing. Which means he had made it his business to do it. He had made an art of writing. But he had made a business of success. Selective Americans respected him for some of the finest writing in English in the first half of the twentieth century. The great majority of Americans respected him for his success. Unlike Nathanael West, who was spared by failure, Papa was gored by success. He lingered on the bloody horn of it. He loved it. He loved to suffer it. And so the books diminished. Never again would the body of work after World War II compare with the work before it. We are not saying no more good work. But when a man can write no better, think no better, know no more, after he is thirty-five than before, especially a man with the unique artistic equipment of Hemingway, are we not entitled, even obligated, again to ask, why? What happened? Why isn't Hemingway Tolstoy? Why isn't Fitzgerald Turgenev? Why isn't Nelson Algren or Norman Mailer Dostoevski? Why are the odds so high that James Jones will never write another *From Here to Eternity,* that Ralph Ellison will never write another *Invisible Man,* just as Richard Wright never wrote another *Native Son?* Why did the mighty river of Thomas Wolfe flood up too soon and overflow its banks?

The history of our literature is strewn with question marks. Or are they gaffs for hauling the poor fish out of water to display in our trophy rooms? The tragedy of Scott Fitzgerald, thanks to a kind of literary overkill, is in danger of becoming one of our great American clichés. Although his success-in-failure, failure-in-success, is understandably fascinating, like a literate terror movie. But the tragedy of Hemingway may cut even deeper because he pitied Fitzgerald for having fallen from grace, from the Number One Cloud. He was condescending toward Fitzgerald, the man who had loaned him money in Paris, had championed his early work, and had even set him up with his own publisher, Scribner's, after Hemingway had expressed the hope that he could be rescued from what he considered his second-class "Jew publishers." In Fitzgerald's own words, when they met after a long separation, "Ernest spoke with the authority of success, and I with the authority of failure."

But exactly how was Hemingway succeeding and Fitzgerald failing? Scott was having a bad time of it, that was true. His wife's mind was breaking down, as were his finances, and his first novel of the thirties, *Tender Is the Night,* was strangely unloved and unsold. So Scott was, both in Hemingway's eyes and the eyes of the public, "failing," while Hemingway was still hot, a big name sought after by national magazines and columnists. But in the middle thirties, could anyone say that Hemingway's work was that much superior to Fitzgerald's? Taking two novels of the same period, was *To Have and Have Not* a towering success and *Tender* a miserable failure? My own judgment, if one must choose one against the other, is now and was at the time on the side of *Tender Is the Night.* But we are not considering literary judgments *per se.* We are considering the American dilemma of big-time success and its opposite face, abysmal failure. Hemingway was the symbol of success because that is how he and the public considered him, the heavyweight champion of American letters. Their dramatic juxtaposition had nothing to do with their respective merits. Hemingway, by his own admission, was Number One, on top of the heap, and poor Fitzgerald was a former contender now no longer rated. Hemingway, the front runner, seemed to despise Fitzgerald for "failing." And Scott's mind was divided. Despite the dog days, he knew he was good; floating in the debris of the shipwreck, he clung to the floating log of faith in his own shattered talent. To intimates he even confided that as a novelist he thought he had certain gifts superior to Ernest's. But the stigma of failure was a heavy collar around his neck, and his old hero and tormentor, friend and rival, did not make it easier by flaunting his Number Oneness.

Having cock-of-the-walked it all of his life, Hemingway could not help Fitzgerald and could not help himself. You could take that Oak Park, Illinois, boy out of America, expatriate him in exotic places, Paris and Spain and Cuba, but you could never take the Middle American spirit of "We're Number One!" out of the artist. If you think of it globally, you get the full impact of the absurdity concealing the tragedy. Can you imagine E. M. Forster, say, or Graham Greene, calling out to his critics and his public, "I'm Number One!"? Or Octavio Paz in Mexico raising one finger and shouting "¡Numero Uno!"? Or even the latest winner of the Goncourt Prize calling out, "Je suis Numéro Un!"? No, this Big Daddy-Number One business may lap over on other cultures but it is strictly an American product like No-Doz and Coca-Cola. And Hemingway didn't invent it, he is simply a dramatic and convenient symbol for the phenomenon. In a "Number One" culture, where our presidents are fond of pointing with pride to their country as the richest and most powerful as well as the most benevolent upon the earth, it is to be expected that our literature will become a product to be sold to the public like cigarettes and rented cars—for Hertz read Hemingway while the newest discovery Charlie Avis admits he's Number Two, but makes up for that deficiency by trying harder.

Is not the entire concept of a "Best Seller List," which a Hemingway must continue to dominate if he is not to turn suicidal, an American monstrosity? Has the muse not become a prisoner of Madison Avenue and the Number One syndrome when even the august *New York Times* dutifully hands down its best sellers numbered one to ten with a kind of biblical authority as if they had been inscribed by Moses on stone?* And of course the joker in this deck, as everyone in the book business knows, is that these lists are shaky educated guesses at best, drawn from the opinions of clerks "on the floor" in a dozen stores around the country. Publishers know that it is no great task to influence them—the whole thing is a kind of make-shift literary roulette with everyone watching to see if an Irwin Shaw or a Jim Jones or a Mailer (or yes, this writer also) "makes the top ten." Like pop songs or the "most active" issues on the market. In drugstores all over America, book buyers know to select only what that Best Seller List has told them "America is reading." Must we turn faucets on writers, making them "hot" or "cold"? Or think of them in terms of commodities with fluctuating prices? For instance, a recent review in *The New York Times* observes, "Though Mann is still the representative modern German writer, his public stock has fallen very low, lower far than Hemingway's ever dropped."

Granted that many writers, let us even say most, could not care less about their opening and closing daily bids, still we have seen what this kind of pressure, this hyped-up commercialism making "folk heroes" of some and "bums" of others, has done to some of our finest writers. The kind of excessive adulation that both Hemingway and Fitzgerald received, and that clearly gave them great joy and great pain, was something they had to suffer and cope with. Each in his different way had to pay a steep price in wounded vanity and loss of self-confidence. Each was competing not only with the best he had to offer (which is the positive form of artistic competition) but with the image each one had created or had encouraged the public to create for him. England has its literary lions who may be exhibited as prize guests at cocktail parties where the Fancy match martinis with the Intelligentsia. But that isn't the same as being quoted

* Since this was written, *The New York Times Book Review* has reflected its sensitivity to this argument by moving its "Best Seller List" to second position beneath "New and Recommended," a step in the right direction.

in Leonard Lyons' gossip column or appearing on the Johnny Carson Show. Of course we have our Salingers who work in secrecy, our Malamuds and Joyce Carol Oateses who work in relative privacy. But we also have our Mailers who are not satisfied to comment brilliantly on the American scene but feel some American compulsion to leap up onto the stage and grab the microphone. When we were covering the Liston-Patterson heavyweight title fight together some years ago, Norman expressed this hunger quite nakedly. He told me he was going to usurp Sonny Liston's place in the winner's circle at the press conference. I questioned whether this would be a dignified move for a novelist. Should the author of *The Naked and the Dead* and *The Deer Park* have to compete with the prizefight champion of the world? Norman's answer was a revelation. Since he had not had a successful novel in some years (and of course, like so many gifted young Americans, had never been able to equal his first great success), he felt driven to execute a "caper" (I believe that was the word he chose) that would help to keep him in the public eye.

Mailer, you may say, is a special case, a writer flowing and overflowing with brilliance, as highly praised as any post-World War II novelist in America, who yet feels the desperate need to write and act out those "advertisements for myself." But is he atypical or, like the Hemingway whose social behavior he emulates, just more typical, more of a prototype of the American writer in all his outer-directed hunger? Needing to be Number One, is he not quite secure enough to rest on his literary laurels, even though they would entitle him to membership in a select group of American writers endowed with honesty, originality, and intellect? No, that is never enough for our Number Ones. They must go dashing up and down the countryside brandishing their lances and charging windmills like Don Quixotes. Or rather, charging television stations, mass meetings, and banquets. To my embarrassment, and because I am also indelibly American, I sometimes do it myself. I am not putting Hemingway and Mailer down. I am putting the breed

under the light. Is there any other culture in which showbiz
and bookbiz are so overlapped? These days how easily Erich
Segal jogs from one to the other. And in reverse how effort-
lessly the stars of show business turn out their obligatory books.
Most of them are ghost-written potboilers. Occasionally an appealing personal quality comes through. But they are still
reflections of an age which has merged showbiz and bookbiz
into one razzle-dazzle popularity contest. Has anybody truly
read Mr. Segal's little book? I have never heard its contents
seriously discussed. What I have heard at scores of literary
soirees is the number of sales it has enjoyed and the box-office
records of the film from which the novelette was drawn. Understandably the engaging literary schizophrene from Yale put
more energy into running the Boston marathon than novelizing
his contempo-movie. And seeming to be a fairly well-balanced
young chap, he may be the first to laugh at his success in putting
one over on the bookbiz world. Still, regardless of the literary
matter of this first concoction, the phenomenon of its instant
celebrity moves it into the focus of our concern. Only in America is there the kind of instant success that greeted *Love Story*.
It is the kind of whirlwind that sweeps over heroes and hacks,
pathfinders and mediocrities. Instant celebrity is an excessively
catholic god. Classics and trash have become instant successes
creating instant celebrities. We have Jacqueline Susann and
Philip Roth, Harold Robbins and Eudora Welty. The Number
One-ism that changes literature to bookbiz would be merely an
amusing sidelight on creative life if I had not observed, again
and again, its traumatic effect on serious people. Not on *all*
writers I have known, obviously, but on enough of them to
suggest that it is more than an individual or eccentric problem.
I have known some writers who have found the strength to
stand off super-success and its strangely similar other face,
super-failure. But I cannot think of any who accomplished this
easily, or without a struggle. And even successful struggle can
be debilitating, distracting, a drain on resources. It obviously
takes something out of you to have to holler "I'm Number

One!" or "Gee, I wish I were Number One again!" or "I'll be Number One when I'm dead, you rascals you!" or even, "Do I care if I'm Number One as long as I still write good?"

Number One-ism is like a hand over one's face blotting out the sun. Hemingway loomed so large that he tended not by talent alone but by the force of his personality to overpower formidable contemporaries. Like John Dos Passos. It is true that Dos Passos' fictional powers seemed to desert him in the forties and fifties after his masterful trilogy, *U.S.A.*, was behind him. Still I believe the impact of Hemingway obscured for a new generation the enormous contribution of Dos Passos. Young people in the fifties and sixties were still very much aware of Hemingway, even though, as *The New York Times* had observed, his stock was falling. But Dos Passos' stock seemed to have disappeared from the Big Board entirely. Out-Number-One'd by Hemingway and replaced as a social novelist by John Steinbeck, his reputation had fallen into a sunset time. And yet *U.S.A.* was the first twentieth-century American novel that dared to take all of America as its hero and antihero. As an experiment in both form and content Alfred Kazin has compared it to the Wright Brothers' airplane and Frank Lloyd Wright's first office buildings. And Sartre has said that he regards Dos Passos as the greatest writer of our time. There we go with those superlatives again. The truth is, how does one compare Dos Passos to Hemingway to Fitzgerald to Wolfe to Faulkner to Steinbeck to Nathanael West? Can you really rate them like this year's tennis rankings? Trouble is, we Americans have a compulsion to rate the unratable. We have a passion for lists. It is the driven pragmatist in us. Is there any other culture in which the words *winner* and *loser* carry such an apocalyptic force? Somewhere along the line, while Hemingway was desperately trying to hang on to his championship—like an aging Joe Louis trying to hold off a surging Rocky Marciano—Dos Passos was slipping down into the netherworld of losers. Again we ask, is this not only in America? *U.S.A.* was a profoundly ambitious novel. By contrast, *The Great Gatsby* and

The Sun Also Rises are much smaller though invaluably Flaubertian works of art. Neither Number One nor Number Ten, Dos Passos is simply a writer who made a pivotal and heroic contribution to our literary storehouse. Only when we succeed in defining rather than rating Dos Passos, Anderson, Fitzgerald, Wolfe, Faulkner, O'Hara, Lewis, Farrell, Wright, Algren, Salinger, Mailer, Bellow, or their successors in public favor and disfavor, will we truly be able to savor them without spoiling the taste with limitless adulation or limited deprecation.

Saul Bellow is a case in point. Is it not enough to admire him for his intelligence and devotion to his craft? But a recent profile in *The New York Times Book Review* hails him as "the premier American novelist: the best writer we have . . ." Etc. Number One-ism rides again! Bellow happens to be a serious man, academy-based, lacking, happily for him, the kind of personality that lights up and fires off rockets at the touch of a hyperbolical match. His sense of proportion should immunize him against the disease of Number One-ism that has infected so many of his peers and predecessors. Still, how does it serve him, and how does it serve American letters, to adulate rather than appreciate his qualities?

What is so funny-sad about this Number One business is that each generation must make its judgment on the basis of so imperfect a scale that nuggets of true gold are sometimes outweighed, for a lifetime or two, by fool's gold. Stendhal, the arrogant little dandy, ached at the popular success of writers he (and perhaps only Balzac) knew to be his inferiors. Overlooked by contemporaries not ready for flinty cynicism and social satire in the rococo days of the Bourbons, he predicted, almost to the year, the renascence a century later of *The Red and the Black* and his other great works.

In my library is a work on Russian authors by Prince Kropotkin, written at the turn of the century. It devotes a third of its contents to Goncharov, who shares honors with Tolstoy and Turgenev as major novelists. Appended to the book is a list of "minor writers." Awarded one patronizing paragraph is Dostoevski, praised mainly for his realistic descriptions of Russian poverty. In the current *New York Times Encyclopaedia*'s list of more than fifty major novelists, Goncharov goes unmentioned. Nor will you find his name in a subsequent list of more than five hundred other noted writers. Goncharov, a titan in his own time, no longer exists, except as a quirk of literary history. But ninety years after his death Dostoevski has become the sun from which the most ambitious of our novelists draw their heat and their light.

We cite these outgoing and incoming literary tides not merely because they are cultural curiosities but because they throw a surgical light on the disease of Number One-ism. Consider Melville's experience with a public that bestows its favors like an ardent but fickle mistress. In his first season of success, when he was still in his twenties, Herman Melville enjoyed a nineteenth-century version of instant celebrity. The acclaim for his South Sea adventure novels, *Omoo* and *Typee,* quickly established him as a Find, a welcome Number One for the 1840s. *White Jacket,* a sensational exposé of the brutalizing life of an ordinary seaman in our four-masted Navy, anticipated the muckraking journalism of the twentieth century and added to Melville's fame and notoriety.

Then poor Herman seems to have committed the popular sin of stretching his literary muscles and his moral imagination. He wrote *Moby-Dick.* Hindsight makes this all cruelly ridiculous, but *Moby-Dick* was poorly received. After exotic manuscripts like *Omoo* and *Typee, Moby-Dick* seemed to critics and the reading public of the 1850s wordy, obtuse, and philosophically murky. As with Stendhal's *The Red and the Black,* critics and readers simply had yet to be informed that it was a masterpiece. With *Moby-Dick* began a fall from public favor that drove Melville out of the writing profession before he was forty. His genius dimly survived in privately printed poems and personal diaries. For twenty years he drudged on the docks of New York as an obscure customs inspector. Only toward the end of his life did he surface for a last-gasp work of fiction, the now famous and exploited *Billy Budd*. As far as literary history is concerned, from the 1850s to the 1920s, Herman Melville was a nonperson. And then suddenly, forty years ago, Melville was resurrected, thanks largely to Lewis Mumford, who brought him back from a premature grave with the publication of his invaluable biography. And of course we all know the result. After two dead seasons in his middle and advancing years, Melville was back with a vengeance, back to Number One again, his *Moby-Dick* finally acclaimed as nothing less than the greatest novel in the entire march of American literature. The eminent professors who had scorned *Moby-Dick* for three generations now proclaimed it the *War and Peace* of our national letters. The despised and neglected Melville came into his posthumous glory. He rode a flood tide of adulation that has never ebbed. If only the bitter customs official standing out there in the cold of a North River winter could know the ceaseless outpouring of praise, analysis, interpretation, that has run his reputation to the top of the mast. What a mean joke his success makes of the great game of musical chairs that American critics, English teachers, and their slavish public never tire of playing.

It is of course excusable to fail to recognize a masterpiece. *Moby-Dick* is not only a great work, it is also overwritten, tendentious, and obsessively detailed. Great chunks of nonfiction are imbedded in it, a practice Tolstoy employed with controversial effect in *War and Peace*. Melville's contemporaries did not see the trees because they had been transformed into masts and did not see the forest because it had been transmuted as a wilderness of the soul. The critical fault lay, then as now, in taking the works one by one, to hail one as "great" and deplore its successors as woolly failures. Obviously, we see now that the same talent was at work in Melville's "flops" as in his "hits," the same powers of observation, the same intellect, the same richness of prose, the same searching conscience. Only these qualities were deepened, became more sophisti-

cated and tortured as he matured from his best-selling late
twenties to his increasingly self-appraising and value-
challenging thirties. The price he paid for this upward struggle
was an unconscionable indifference on the part of his erstwhile
public. While he may have had his Hawthorne, as Stendhal had
his Balzac, there was no significant body of criticism and read-
ership to sustain the neglected Melville, to say, "We who set
him up so high in 1846 must at least bear with him and—even
if we cannot follow or understand him lately—*read* him in 1856.
Otherwise are we not failing the fresh new writer we welcomed
so heartily when he was giving us *Omoo, Typee, Mardi,* and
Redburn?" The fact that *Moby-Dick* is now required reading
in every American literature course and *Redburn* unknown except to Melville scholars is not really the point. If the enthu-
siasts for *Mardi* and *Redburn* had thought of the whole writer
and had not pieced him off book by book, hit by flop, *Moby-
Dick* and *Pierre* might at last have been read in truer
perspective, and with kindlier eyes.

The plight of Melville and the tragic lag between his years of
darkness and the sunrise in his pocket—in his tomb!—are the
very essence of the American Story of Success in Failure and
Failure in Success. Or think of Jack London. Desperately poor,
his cheap room papered with rejection slips in his early twenties, then famous only a few years later, he became a hive of
contradictions: a nouveau-riche socialist, his novels whiplashed
between Marxism and Nietzscheism, their proletarian material
warring with his theme of a master race. Spoiled, frustrated and
confused, he went plunging down to neglect and suicide at the
age of forty.

A year or so ago, a small tempest raged around the embarrassingly short run of Edward Albee's latest play—titled, with
special significance for this introduction, *All Over.* Albee's
play was graced with Colleen Dewhurst and Jessica Tandy, and
was directed by John Gielgud. Its opening was heralded as one
of the major events of the season. But it was savagely knocked
down by the majority of critics and after a brief run was

counted out. Max Lerner, deep-thinker-in-residence for the *New York Post,* has this to say about the collision Albee had just suffered as he went tooling along the expressway of American fame and fortune:

> The trouble with being in Albee's position—this was true once also of O'Neill, Hellman, Miller, Tennessee Williams—is that the critics and audiences want you to strike twelve each time you write a new play. They love the sweet smell of a sure-fire hit. In our witless concern only with the individual piece of work we forget that a new play is part of an ongoing arc of development.
>
> We are too hurried to study its place in the arc. If O'Neill were alive, and had just written and produced *Moon for the Misbegotten,* or *More Stately Mansions,* most critics would cut it and him into little pieces and say he had become the club bore. But O'Neill was what he was because each play was neither victory nor defeat, in a continuing war with himself.

Albee fought back from his house high above the beach at Montauk, where he was bathing his wounds in his swimming pool, playing off his frustrations on his tennis court, soothing his hurts in his sauna bath, surrounded by sensitive and sympathetic friends, the sculpture of Henry Moore, and the sound of the surf on his private beach. Outwardly enjoying the trappings of success, how many Number Ones have fought back from similar fortresses, or retreats, hoping to drive off the furies that lay siege to the castle of their reputation? Albee was speaking for Melville and James Branch Cabell and Scott Fitzgerald and Tennessee Williams and everybody else lifted high and dropped hard, when he said, "There is a syndrome in this country. The critics set somebody up, maybe too soon—underline *maybe*—and then they take pleasure . . . in knocking him down." A close friend and theater associate elaborated: "The reaction to Edward's play has been exceptional. A major work by a major playwright—you just don't kick it down the toilet that way."

Albee's play was all over before I had a chance to see it and I felt cheated. Whether I would have sided with those who thought it was boring and inactive, or with those who thought it was haunting and deeply moving, I have no idea. Nor does it really matter. What matters is that an Albee play or a Williams play or a play by any writer of proved distinction, embellished by players of distinction, deserves to run long enough for at least every theatergoer who wants to see it to do so, so that he can find a place for it in the *body of work*. That is the only way, as Lerner has said, that an established writer should be judged, according to "an ongoing arc of development." I suspect that the reason we do not judge writers this way, the reason we seem to take special delight in crowning them before they are ready and dethroning them before they are finished, is that we are a nation with a history that is still very short, we are in the main a pragmatic people better at doing than contemplating, strong on know-how and suspicious of tradition. And so we dig success, instant success, we look for results and are impatient with processes. In Hollywood they like to say you are only as good as your last picture, and this quick count is also used to flag down front-running careers in other arenas of our creative life. Playwrights, novelists, and to a lesser extent even poets are victimized by the psychology of *what-was-your-last-hit?*

Most American writers agree that the authors in countries beyond our borders are treated with a deeper, unseasonal respect. Juan Rulfo, for instance, is always introduced in Mexican artistic circles as "one of our most important novelists," although the small novel for which he is best known, *Pedro Paramo,* was published in the fifties. If he were in New York, or in a university town for that matter, Sr. Rulfo would undoubtedly be asked, "What have you done lately?" A novelist currently on the best-seller list was complaining to me recently that one of the occupational hazards of literary cocktail parties is to be asked not about his work in general but, "What have you got on the fire now?" All of us who toil in the overlapping fields of literature and bookbiz are familiar with this question. You may have worked your heart out on a book for the past three years. You may need time to lie fallow and just think. No matter. Next time you find yourself up against the cocktail wall you will hear yourself trying to cope with that superbly and maddeningly American question, "What have you got on the fire *now?*"

In a sense it might be considered a flattering question, an indication of your public's immediate interest in your creative activity. Fine, we would say, but too *immediate* and too *active*. There is something about the question that does not provide sufficient breathing room. Something about the question is wired, painfully, to our conception of the Seasons of Success.

In the span of my life I have known a great many writers, having been drawn to the species in my Hollywood adolescence as noted earlier, and having been privileged to know some of the standouts, some of them intimately, some of them very well, some of them well enough to consider them my friends, and a few even well enough to recognize as my enemies. As I think about them, in the context of Stendhal and Melville and Dostoevski, as I contemplate the lives of Sinclair Lewis, William Saroyan, Scott Fitzgerald, Nathanael West, Charles Jackson, John O'Hara, Clifford Odets, Dorothy Parker, Ernest Hemingway, Thomas Heggen, James Baldwin, Norman Mailer, James Jones, Irwin Shaw, Tennessee Williams, John Steinbeck, William Faulkner, and others whose paths have crossed with mine —I find myself dividing their careers into Seasons of Success. First is the spring season of early success, like Fitzgerald's and Odets's, Saroyan's and Heggen's. The summer season, when men who had put in their apprenticeship, like London and Lewis and Steinbeck, enjoyed the full flowering of their talents and their public's response. The autumn, when talent is still manifestly there, though the public has begun to grow cold. Then the long hard winter of discontent that settled over Melville and Lewis, Farrell and Steinbeck. And finally the second spring, the second coming, when the bulb buried in the ground and unsensed by ignorant age or innocent youth bursts forth again in glorious reaffirmation like tulips and daffodils. The second spring of Herman Melville and Scott Fitzgerald and the posthumous first spring of Nathanael West.

Of the many friends or acquaintances mentioned above, and the others that have come to mind because they had their season or two, or may again, I have chosen six whose life and work exemplify the changing Seasons of Success that have afflicted all the writers I have known. These are not essays but assays, efforts to place my memory of these men at the service not merely of literary history but of literary continuity. One never conquers the winds, but the better we understand them the better able we are to cope with them. If the winds of success blow too harshly around our heads, or conversely fail to blow at all, I offer these reminiscences as a protective shelter. I dedicate them to the ASPCA, since, especially in America, that final letter should stand for Authors as well as Animals.

I. ❖ ❖ SINCLAIR LEWIS
Big Noise from Sauk Centre

"I've already done my best work . . . *Babbitt* will probably be rated my best book."

—SINCLAIR LEWIS, 1926, AGE 41

On becoming the first American writer to win the Nobel Prize (1930):
"This is the end of me . . . fatal . . . I cannot live up to it."

SINCLAIR LEWIS may have been a little too broad and social for the narrow-gauge, introspective fifties and the "Wow! —Now!" existentialist sixties that turned their backs on him. But he blew a lot of fresh air into the musty corners of Victorianism that were still waiting for a thorough vacuum cleaning in the days of Harding and Coolidge. Lewis was fresh in every way, really a fresh guy in the best no-nonsense American style. That was my opinion of his best work, the half dozen books that built his monument from 1920 to 1930, and when I met him under rather odd circumstances in the middle thirties I found him to be much of a piece with his work.

Nearly forty years ago, when Lewis published *It Can't Happen Here,* I was at Dartmouth College in Hanover, New Hampshire, editor of our daily paper and, naturally, bristling with antifascism. Lewis had endeared himself to our fathers with *Main Street, Babbitt, Arrowsmith, Elmer Gantry,* and *Dodsworth,* but now in 1935, the year of Mussolini and Hitler abroad, of Huey Long and Father Coughlin at home, the literary terror from Sauk Centre was reestablishing himself with our embattled Depression Generation. *It Can't Happen Here* was the high sign we had been waiting for: Lewis was one of ours. A third of a century later the totalitarian horrors, American style, that Lewis projected for us in the Huey-like form of Senator Windrip may seem at best a little provincial, at worst a manic-panic burlesque. Today even the right-wing banquet-circuit wit and wisdom of Spiteful Spiro suggests that when and if the dreaded *It* lowers its nose cone over us, it will have to be packaged and sweetened to majority taste. But in those days of Coughlin's "Social Justice," Pelley's Silver Shirts, the Brown Shirts of Fritz Kuhn and the Black Shirts of Detroit, Senator

Windrip seemed all too real. Having already shaken the middle-class conscience of our parents, the creator of a homegrown American dictator knew exactly how to find and squeeze the nerve of political indignation in a new generation of readers who had begun to refer to themselves, with graveyard humor, as Veterans of Future Wars.

My own enthusiasm for Lewis, and for his welcome commitment to the antifascist cause, was brewed to the boiling point when the avant-garde poet and Proust scholar, Professor Ramon Guthrie, a close friend of Lewis's in those Paris Left Bank days ten years earlier, asked me if I realized that "Red," as he called him, was living just over the mountain, near Woodstock, Vermont, an easy hour's drive. Practically a neighbor!

The following weekend I decided to combine the pleasure of a day-off excursion with some editorial business by driving over to call on Sinclair Lewis and interviewing him for the school paper. Most of my English professors, along with a pride of sophomore lions, put it down as a foolhardy mission. Lewis had become virtually a recluse. His ill temper was notorious. I would find a small army of servants, secretaries, bodyguards, and castle dragons to run me off. "So what's the worst that can happen to me?" the boy in me countered. "After all, he can't eat me!"

"On the contrary," said an aging bachelor professor of English who specialized in obscure modern poetry and acidic notes on our earnest literary efforts, "I am under the distinct impression that roasted undergraduate is one of the favorite dishes on his menu. I'm not joking, Schulberg. I wouldn't risk it."

Nevertheless, that Friday afternoon I found my way across the White River and into the trees protecting a large white clapboard estate house a few miles beyond Woodstock. I took a deep breath and knocked on the door. I had to knock several times before anyone answered. Then the door swung open and a tall, skinny man with long arms and legs and one of the ugliest faces I had ever seen looked out and barked at me, "Well? What d'ya want?"

A small voice that sounded stuck in its throat hesitatingly identified me as the editor of the Dartmouth College daily and a friend of Professor Guthrie's.

"What the hell are you stammering for?" he barked again.

"I'm stammering because . . . I stammer," I stammered. "Makes me sound more frightened than I—I really am."

"Huh. All right. Come in."

The house was warm and inviting and lonely and empty. There was a wonderful, long living room lined with books and looking out through a wall of glass onto a seemingly endless terrace that dropped down in a series of broad, grassy steps. I kept looking around, surprised to find no one else in sight. No servants, no secretaries, no wife. "Mrs. Lewis"—that was the well-known Dorothy Thompson—"is off on a lecture tour," he answered my silent question. "Wanna drink?"

I followed Mr. Lewis into the kitchen to help get the ice and the mixings. On the way back I paused to look at the shelves of European editions of Lewis novels. I felt a sense of awe and youthful envy. Then we went out on the veranda overlooking those grass terraces, and started drinking together. It was easy talking because we shared, from opposite ends of the telescope of age, an enthusiasm for Ramon Guthrie. "I'm crazy about Ramon," Lewis said in a voice rather loud for an audience of one. "He c'n do 'em all—paint, fly, write novels, poetry . . . The only thing I thought he couldn't do is hold down a job in a conservative New England college like Dartmouth. You know, I got 'im the job. Never thought he'd hold it more'n a year or two. Good old Ramon! Of that whole nutty crowd over in Paris he was one of the few who had genius. Only trouble was, he was a genius in so many different directions. If he ever settles down to one, he'll take it all."*

* In the winter of his life, after half a century of undeserved obscurity, Ramon Guthrie is enjoying a late-blooming season of success, just as Lewis had predicted. His book-length poems, *Graffiti* and *Maximum Security Ward*, have established him as one of the most original and pungent poets of our time.

We went in and refilled our glasses and I paid my courteous and sincere obeisance to the Lewis novels that I had enjoyed. They were books, I tried to say, that had made me laugh uncomfortably at the cultural wasteland of Middle America. "Oh, George Babbitt isn't such a bad guy," Lewis said. "Actually I kinda like him." He seemed pleased, but not particularly anxious to talk about the old ones. The only book alive for him at that moment was *It Can't Happen Here*. I addressed a self-conscious, or, rather, socially conscious, tribute to the book: how important it was that an author of Lewis's stature—our first and then our only Nobel Prize winner—had taken so firm and uncompromising an antifascist position. That was the way we talked in those unalienated days. "We've just formed a campus chapter of the League Against War and Fascism—Ramon is one of our faculty advisers—and *It Can't Happen Here* has given us some valuable ammunition, Mr. Lewis," I said. Eased by the highballs and his informality, I was hardly stammering any more.

"Oh hell, call me Red," he said. And then completely ignoring my mouthful of social significance, he said, "That Charlie Coughlin, he's really something, isn't he? Christ, but he gives me a kick!" Just thinking about it made him laugh, raucously, and for a moment or two I actually did not realize that he was referring to *our* Father Coughlin. For us at the college, particularly in our left-liberal League Against War and Fascism, the mention of Father Coughlin and his "Christian Front" was an automatic starter setting off violent vibrations of political hatred and militant anger. His name stood for demagogic panaceas, anti-Semitism, a virulent cloth-protected fascism spreading out from Detroit in all directions. To my surprise, and rather to my dismay, Lewis was unable to take him that seriously. To his quizzical eyes, Coughlin was just another funny Charlie, like Charlie Chan and Charlie Chase.

Taking stage in the middle of the living room, Lewis delivered an impersonation of Father Coughlin and his radio rabble-rousing that reduced it, or elevated it, to first-rate vaudeville.

I had known some novelists before, mostly those who had come to Hollywood to mend their fortunes, but I had never encountered one who could act out and mime his material this way. The way he took off "Charlie" Coughlin reminded me of once having seen Charlie Chaplin do an impromptu Schickelgruber routine at a party, years before his classic charade as *The Great Dictator*. Looking back it may seem odd to compare the comedic talents of Sinclair Lewis with those of Charlie Chaplin, but on our third highball, as he racked up Coughlin and moved on to Huey Long, William Dudley Pelley, Fritz Kuhn, and our other American would-be Führers, it struck me as an inspired, satirical performance. We made an oddly assorted pair that afternoon. I had been sternly and perhaps immaturely incapable of taking our homegrown Gauleiters lightly, while Red Lewis seemed congenitally incapable of taking them any other way.

Although I had come with a headful of questions, somewhere during the interview—which grew inadvertently into a visit—my host became the more aggressive questioner. The marble workers were on strike in the nearby Rutland-Proctor area, and Lewis—by this time at his insistence I was tentatively calling him "Red"—wanted to know all about it. I had gone over to Proctor to cover the strike for my paper and the series of articles that resulted had, to put it lightly, become something of a *succès de scandale*. The Proctors were an illustrious Dartmouth family known for their generosity to the College. But my report of wives and children of their marble workers freezing and starving had brought to our editorial office halls a surprising overflow of clothing and food parcels from sympathetic faculty members and students. This largesse we dispatched to Proctor by the truckload. But after the first few deliveries, which had caught them by surprise, State troopers—brazenly on the side of the quarry owners—had turned back our convoy. I had been flagged down by deputy sheriffs, local bully boys sworn in for this emergency, and warned to stay the hell out of Proctor and the other embattled quarry towns. In fact, any representative of our school paper was promptly labeled a "Commie" and ordered by the authorities to "get your asses out of Proctor and back across the State line to Dartmouth where you belong!" Only a few miles from where Red was living, I told him, were company towns, feudal in structure and fascist in effect, where indigenous storm troopers were terrorizing foreign-born quarry workers with shotguns, clubs, and patriotic threats. *It Can't Happen Here,* I warned my host with undergraduate zeal, was not only a prophetic book but its dire prophecy was already *happening,* and practically on the doorstep of this luxurious farmhouse.

An eager listener as well as a great talker, Lewis responded with the sharp, staccato questions of a crack reporter, pressing me for *details,* not *theories.* He had a passion for the former, and a loathing for the latter. Now I found myself taking his place, taking stage and pacing up and down that spacious living room as I went on with my story of the boy journalist aiming his sling shot at the all-powerful Goliath of Vermont:

When the *Rutland Herald* prematurely headlined the ending of the strike, a delegation of marble workers had come to our newspaper office to deny it, and we had counterheadlined the strikers' angry attack on the *Herald* story as a company ruse. The marble strikers had hailed ours as the only paper in Vermont or New Hampshire reporting their strike truthfully; conversely, the Proctor Marble Company, the American Legion, the *Rutland Herald* and the *Hanover Gazette,* convinced that dear old Dartmouth was harboring a Communist conspiracy, were crying for our scalps. The president of Dartmouth, Ernest Martin Hopkins, was being flooded with letters from irate alumni, the kindest suggesting that I be "immediately separated from the College," but some preferring that I be strung up for high treason. I had been invited to describe our involvement with the strike on other campuses, had been denounced in the New Hampshire Legislature, and had been politely ordered to come to the State capital to defend myself. At issue, it seemed, was a question then in its infancy: the right of student opinion to involve itself in (rather than merely study) social, economic, and national crises. The novelty of the thing, and perhaps the comedy of a Hollywood producer's son breaking through the Ivy curtain and running the gantlet of company thugs to bring help to the struggling proletariat, was such an odd little footnote to the class struggle that it came to national attention.

It all sounded like the plot of one of those righteous Depression novels then coming into fashion, and Red's reaction was a characteristic amalgam of serious interest and vast amusement. He plied me with good questions and good Scotch and I warmed to my subject, describing the native humor of the quarry miners that I was trying to work into a college play.* Management had warned the workers that if they did not give up their protracted strike, the Proctors would shut down the quarries and move their business to the South, where unionism, civil rights, and other intrusions were simply not tolerated. To which the leader of the marble workers had responded, "Go ahead 'n' move. That's somethin' we been waitin' t' see—you Proctors movin' yer goddamn marble y'selves!"

Red's laugh was like the bark of a seal. He warmed to the idea that the strikers didn't take themselves too seriously. One of the things he despised about fascist movements was their lack of humor. He thought Hitler and Goebbels and the Brown Shirts were able to take over Germany because "the goddamned krauts never had a sense of humor." In spite of the doomsday novel he had just written, he really didn't believe that Americans would fall for the applesauce of a Hitler or a Mussolini. The reason "Hooey" Long had gone as far as he had was that he had never lost touch with the earthy humor of the Louisiana rednecks who took to his slogan, "Every man a king." Red saw the assassination of Long as a sign that tyrants might find the going harder here in America than in Europe, since we were freer of ritual and dogma in a land where the independent, inquiring spirit still survived. He saw hope in the cussed inde-

*Company House, a would-be Odetsian one-acter produced in the Dartmouth Little Theater in 1935.

pendence of the Vermonter, despite the moneyed hierarchy and its hired troopers that I had come up against in Rutland. When I told him about Archibald MacLeish's efforts to rally fellow writers to the strikers' cause,* Red said he wouldn't go anywhere to please Archie MacLeish because he had no use for poets who wrote about Democracy with a capital D. Instead, he wanted to hear more from me about the facts of the case: how much the marble workers earned an hour, how much the marble was sold for, and what kind of profit the Proctors enjoyed?

Sharp questions. And full answers. Another hour passed. It had begun to grow dark. We moved inside and when I saw what the hour was, I told Red I was afraid I had overstayed my welcome. On the contrary, he assured me, he had begun to wonder about this new left-wing "Farrell and Steinbeck" generation and I was the first on-the-hoof example of "whatever the hell this new thing is" that he had a chance to know. I thanked him and said I'd like to drive over again some afternoon. Any time, he said, but if I had no plans for dinner, why not stay on and take potluck with him?

So we drank and talked on. Swapping stories and political notions. Disagreeing now and then, but congenially. Neither one of us was pie-eyed, as we used to say then, but the mood was mellow. He told anecdotes of his now-forgotten early fling with socialism, his adolescent attachment to Upton Sinclair's communal farm and his prewar season of idealism when he was a dues-paying member of the Socialist Party. He scoffed at the young believer he had been when he was twenty-one, a quarter of a century earlier—gently mocking my own condition. He talked of his fascination with hotels, whiskey, people—especially Americans. Like H. L. Mencken, his fellow member in the league against boredom and "boobocracy," Lewis had a

---

* "The cause of the marble workers is in the great tradition of Vermont's struggle for freedom. I believe that the cause should be ours as well." MacLeish jotted this down on a piece of brown paper I have saved to this day.

big love-hate thing going for Americans: "If you wanna write, stay put, stay near what you know best, don't let yourself get trapped over there with the Ritz Bar oh-boy-are-we-having-fun-and-ain't-we-artistic! set. I say 'Write America First.'"

The telephone rang and since he picked it up in the hallway off the living room where we had been sitting and made no effort to lower his characteristically boisterous Midwestern voice, I could eavesdrop unashamedly. I wish I could play it back word for word, as I was able to with some of his literary pronouncements. Alas, John O'Haras come one to a lifetime. But it went something like this:

"Oh, hello dear, where are you now, Philadelphia?" I realized it was his indefatigable lecturer-wife Dorothy Thompson. "Oh fine, I'm awfully glad the talk went so well, yes, I called the plumber and he's coming to fix that leak tomorrow, no, I won't forget to tell him about the powder room too, yes, the painter was here this morning to put on the second coat and the garage looks swell, I think you'll be pleased. Where do you talk tomorrow night? Oh, that's right, Baltimore, fine, dear, fine . . ."

As I listened, I began to hear a different Lewis from the all-powerful, all-confident Nobel Prize winner I had conjured on my way over to Woodstock. I may have been reading too much into it, but on the phone he had sounded subdued almost to the point of subservience. A different, more complicated image had begun to superimpose itself on the bolder and apparently oversimplified one that had first taken form in my hero-worshiping mind. To the authoritative, busy opinion-maker Dorothy Thompson, Sinclair Lewis seemed to have become the man who kept the home fires burning. I found myself wondering if the arrogantly famous figure that had been projected for me was simply a lonely man rather desperate for company and perhaps even for reassurance.

"Dorothy's packing 'em in everywhere she goes!" he was saying with what struck me as forced cheerfulness as he returned to the living room. "Seems like nobody knows what to

think of Adolf and Benito and FDR until she sets 'em straight."
I felt the pride and the sarcasm were about equal measure.
"Come on, let's look in the icebox and see what we can find
for supper."

After dinner there was more talk and whiskey, while we
took turns pacing the big living room and leaning on the clas-
sical white mantel in front of the crackling fire. Red kidded me,
but good-naturedly, about what he called my "sophomore socialism." He said the worst thing about it was that it seemed
to make us "Ivy League Marxists" so damned pompous and
closed-minded. Hell, he said, even Gene Debs didn't carry on
about it the way we young doctrinaires were doing. But then,
he added, Gene Debs was an American original. He admired
men who spoke their minds and took their lumps like Gene
Debs. The way he said it came out as one word, *GeneDebs,*
and it took me some moments to realize that his casual Gene-
Debs was the same man I had thought of in capital letters as
The Great Eugene V. Debs with a Socialist halo around his
head. Red told me of a train ride he and GeneDebs had taken
together, when all the railroad workers had dropped by to
shake their leader's hand, and while I was still marveling at
this, he said, almost in the same breath, that of all the outstand-
ing Americans he had known he thought "the two greatest were
probably Gene and Herbert Hoover." In those years, for most
of us, Hoover was a dirty word. We still called the Depression
shantytowns *hoovervilles.* Hoover was the bloated plutocrat in
the top hat in Gropper's *New Masses* cartoons. So I told Red
that comparing Debs to Hoover was like comparing Joe Louis
to Kingfish Levinsky.* To admire one would be to despise
the other.

Lewis laughed at what he called my innocence and then vig-
orously defended his free-wheeling position. I wasn't sure that
night and I've been uncertain ever since as to whether or not
Red tossed Hoover in with Debs just to get that rise out of me.

* One of our lesser Jewish fistic heroes of the period.

To dent my pretensions, my absolutism. He took a Huck Finn's delight in puncturing balloons. It struck me that he had a wonderfully quick intelligence that was not at all concerned with ideas. If his GeneDebs was an American original, so was my RedLewis. Who else could have taken Father Coughlin strictly as Charlie Coughlin? While my generation, my League Against War and Fascism, was trying to make a whole sociological production out of the Führer-priest and his rabid program of "Social Justice" (for white Christians only). It was personality versus ideology and we were still banging our differences around when the grandfather clock in the hall struck midnight.

By this time my firsthand research on Lewis had enveloped a full eight-hour day plus a few hours' overtime so I apologized for overstaying my welcome and moved toward the door. But there was the drink for the road, and then another, and finally an hour later Red was saying, "It's a helluva long drive over the mountain at this time o' night. Might as well stay over, I've got plenty o' room." So we talked and drank our way into the dawn, and then adjourned until the early afternoon. Saturday was a repetition of Friday, even to the phone calls from the peripatetic Dorothy and his dutifully domestic reports. By Sunday I was definitely the boy who came to dinner. Lewis's luxurious white frame farmhouse had become a home away from home and dormitory life at Dartmouth seemed years ago and far away.

Back in Hanover, I was to discover on my return, my friends had become so anxious about me that they actually had called the police stations in various towns along the way. I was a notoriously erratic driver in those days, given to speed combined with absentmindedness. A wheel had mysteriously disengaged itself from my Model-A Ford on a wild return from a Harvard game. And racing back from Smith one beery dawn that same intrepid vehicle had performed a series of cartwheels in a Vermont tobacco field, somehow leaving the driver more embarrassed than injured. So my classmates expected to hear that I had plunged off the winding mountain road and into the White River.

But all of this time the only risk I was running was from an oversupply of Red's very fine Scotch. By Sunday night we were bosom bottle companions, fairly wallowing in companionability, both acknowledging how well we complemented each other—youth and age, radical and conservative, fledgling writer and world-famous literary figure—both agreeing it was one of the best damned stimulating weekends we could remember. The early hours of Monday morning found us moving on to personal confidences, the quick-witted twenty-year-old dancer back home I wanted to marry, and his various complicated wives and his concern for his young son, Michael. By the time I finally drove away around noon on Monday, feeling like a flagpole sitter coming down from my record seventy-two-hour interview, I remember even feeling a little guilty at leaving poor Red alone, with his wife busy pontificating all over the country. He stood in the doorway and waved me off, a lonely figure against that big empty house.

At Dartmouth the following evening I reported my adventure to Ramon Guthrie, who told me he already had heard of the talkfest from Lewis himself: I had scored a tremendous hit with Red, who instinctively hated or loved people on sight. What Red had not told me—with typical literary slyness, as I was to learn from other authors in time—was that he had been planning a labor novel, and already had done considerable factory and union research under Ramon's guidance. In fact, over the past six years this would-be novel had become something of an obsession with Red, his quest for the great white whale, the big novel of political idealism that seemed constantly to elude him. He had even thought to use Debs as a central figure, and the reason he had not confessed this to me in the course of our long weekend was that much as he admired and almost worshiped Debs, there was something about the subject matter that defied and defeated him. Ramon Guthrie, of course, who knew Red Lewis far better than I, having been close to him both in France and in Vermont, now speculated that his friend suffered from a split social conscience. Genuinely aroused by injustice, he responded to Debs, Sacco and Vanzetti, Clarence Darrow, and Tom Mooney. At the same time the inborn skeptic in him prevented him from making any deep commitment to their causes. In our bibulous discussions far into the night, apparently Lewis had been partly in earnest, reflecting his natural suspicion of any organized causes, and partly baiting and devil's-advocating me to see how well I could defend my position, which in many ways had once been his own, and for which he still held a flickering allegiance.

Now I began to realize something more complicated. I had not quite walked into Mr. Lewis's parlor like the innocent fly I had thought myself. Ramon Guthrie, that gentle, sly, benevolent Machiavelli, concerned for his friend's literary health and wanting to see Red achieve the labor novel that had been frustrating and haunting him so long, saw me as the ideal young catalyst who could recharge Lewis's enthusiasm for this on-again-off-again mission. My involvement with the marble strike —how an upper-middle-class college boy gets drawn into the labor struggle, moving from academic theory to active participation—was the perfect grist for his timely but temperamental mill. I had become, in Red's absorbent mind, the model of the generation coming of age in the depth of the Depression. Red would like me to drop in as often as possible, Ramon said, more or less to sit for my literary portrait.

Flattered and intrigued, I drove over to Woodstock a number of times after that. Red seemed to be moving vaguely left again in his own highly individualistic way, and I threw all my missionary zeal into encouraging him. Ramon Guthrie was delighted with the progress I seemed to be making. Admittedly a hard-shell skeptic, Red Lewis was prone to question any social movement, even one as all-embracing as the New Deal. But Ramon thought he saw signs of his famous friend's gradual reconversion to a more humanitarian, socially engaged point of view. Beginning to pierce his armor of iconoclasm, I now sensed in Lewis a kindness, a genuine affection even for the people he pretended to despise. Although Mencken was often considered his mentor—his "antisoul brother," we might call him today—there was hidden in Lewis a love of humanity clearly not shared by the bourgeois-baiting curmudgeon from Baltimore. I did my youthful best to tap this hidden spring. I told him human-interest stories of the marble workers' lives that overlapped with his memories of Debs and the railroad strikers. I knew his loathing for hypocrisy and I evoked the smug college majority, those children of the well-to-do who studied Social Problems in the abstract while an honest-to-god social crisis was right under their noses but somehow beyond their sight. I reminded him how generous the Proctors were, as benefactors of the College, while refusing to give an inch in their negotiations with their underpaid marble workers. I tried to put this in my own words, without resorting to the Marxist jargon that the *New Masses* and the other Communist organs had borrowed from the prose style of Stalin and Eastern Europe. I didn't mention "the toiling masses" and I carefully avoided "surplus labor value," a concept from *Das Kapital* I had never fully digested anyway. It seemed to be working. Red, that fantastic talker, seemed to be listening. He even agreed to accompany me to Proctor, talk with the miners, and lend his name to their cause.

When I thought he was ready I suggested to Lewis, rather tentatively, that he come over and speak at Dartmouth. We—us liberals, deep thinkers, and social philosophers—had a long-hair discussion group called the Junto, modeled on Benjamin Franklin's old philosophical circle, and I thought it would be a fine idea if Lewis would lead a group discussion on "Fascism and the Novel." Somewhat to my surprise, Red accepted. Enthusiastically. If all the Hanover undergraduates were like his new young friend, his manner now seemed to suggest, he was ready to embrace them all. In addition there was his insatiable curiosity. What were these children of the Depression and our

spreading fascist wars *really* like? By this time Red had begun
to conceive of a young Ivy League leftist as the hero of his
labor novel, in fact had decided to broaden his work from a
strictly labor to a "hopeful new generation" approach. It seemed
his search for the "big novel of political idealism" at last was
coming into focus.

On the campus the coming of Sinclair Lewis was considered
quite a coup. I was congratulated even by a few of the varsity
football intelligentsia, who promised to be on hand for this
celebrated occasion. I served as chairman and by way of introduction told the now legendary story of "my weekend with
that ferocious recluse, Sinclair Lewis." Red chuckled appre-
ciatively, the audience laughed and smiled with him and we
were all one happy, mutually admiring family. Red did his
Charlie Coughlin routine, and then his Huey Long, and quoted
from his fictionalized Senator Windrip, and our young high-
domes of the Junto were amused. But as he went on with his
vaudeville, almost exactly the same act he had played to an
audience of one on my first visit to Woodstock, I grew a little
uneasy. I knew my fellow-members and I could read their faces.
This was too serious a matter for spoofing. They were waiting
for the Nobel Prize winner to say something Profound and
Socially Significant about Fascism. Instead, Lewis wound up
with a well-told jest. I asked if there were any questions.

Alas, there were: those deep, theory-ridden, humorless,
classroom-scented questions that can spring only from the
mind of the teen-age intellectual elite.

Did Mr. Lewis realize that fascism was not an isolated, historical phase but the final, inevitable, decadent, death-rattle
stage of capitalism?

Mr. Lewis cleared his throat and muttered something about
not having to be a social scientist. He was just a goddamn novelist.

But how could Mr. Lewis be so politically naïve as not to
relate his novel on fascism to this final stage of capitalism in
which the crumbling democratic façade reveals the decadent

and inevitable violence of dictatorship as the last stand of the ruling class against the revolutionary masses?

Is that a question, or a synopsis of your senior thesis? Mr. Lewis wanted to know.

If this was a storm warning, Lewis's questioners, or rather inquisitors, were sublimely unaware.

Next question: If Mr. Lewis had not studied and absorbed —as obviously he had not—the theories of the leading anti-fascist philosophers, historians, and economists—John Strachey, R. Palme Dutt, Lewis Corey (author of *The Decline and Fall of American Capitalism,* who had lectured to us at Dartmouth a few days earlier in a voice of neo-Marxist doom), if Mr. Lewis had not read Thorstein Veblen and the precursors of the anti-fascist social scientists, then how could Mr. Lewis presume to write a book about fascism, even if it pretends to be a work of fiction?

From my place of honor as chairman I could see Red's jaw going tight. His weirdly mottled poison-ivy complexion seemed to grow even blotchier. His answers grew increasingly mono-syllabic, shot through his teeth. He thought he had written a *novel,* a book to be *enjoyed,* not a goddamn Marxian tract. "And who the hell is R. Palme Dutt? Sounds like a character out of W. C. Fields!" Red got his idea for Senator Buzz Windrip from Charlie Coughlin and Kingfish Huey, he told them, "not from some highly debatable, indigestible, and unpronounceable economic hooey."

Lewis's short-tempered jabs were just what they wanted. My fellow Junto-ites closed ranks and pressed the attack. Is there anything more delicious for the callow intellectual pack than to bring down a literary lion? Or, to shuffle the menagerie deck, for the hagiology hounds to hold the great undoctrinaire stag at bay? I tried to head them off with a diplomatic parry, a safer, more purely literary question of my own. Too late, too late. A sociology honors student locally famous or notorious for his straight A's and his Engelsian zealotry took dead aim on Red with a great bomb of a question, ". . . about Coughlin and silver and the business cycle linked to fascism and the final, repressive stage of capitalist imperialism?" Yes, that was a real fire-bomb of a question, fused with Lewis's ignorance, or defiance if you prefer, of economic theory and political cant.

"You little son of a bitch!" he answered. "All of you! Young sons o' bitches! You c'n all go to hell!"

There went my author, stomping out on those long, stilt-like legs. Exit Nobel Prize winner. A pox on Hands Across the Generations!

Some twenty minutes after the debacle, I followed Red to Ramon Guthrie's snug house across the Connecticut River in Norwich, Vermont. The fire in our honored guest was far from subsiding. In fact he had been stoking it with generous helpings of alcohol. With a tall Scotch in his hand he was telling the room, in that bellicose Middle American voice of his, exactly what he thought of those goddamn supercilious snot-nose know-it-all book-stupid theory-ridden little bastards. Oh ho, would he fix their wagons! *Now* he knew what this young generation was like, the little smart-ass sons o' bitches! He was just lucky he had found out in time. Oh, those young smart-aleck Xz#"&*'s . . . It was our Nobel Prize winner at his most emphatic if somewhat redundant self.

Thus was my missionary work undone. Back to Woodstock roared the literary lion, to lick his wounds and—Ramon Guthrie can substantiate this—revise his attitude and his book just as he had threatened. Out of this spleen came *The Prodigal Parents*—alas, one of the lesser efforts of Sinclair Lewis, a furious larruping of the young, cocksure, left-wing, out-of-kilter generation that *thinks* it knows more than its parents and is sadly and unforgivably mistaken. The hero of this unhappily shallow little novel was "Fred Cornplow," the name a giveaway to the heavy-handed and ill-conceived travesty in which the elder Cornplows are betrayed by the radical irresponsibility of their children. The Cornplows, whom Lewis sets up as American paragons, are comic-book Rotarians, rural patriots who seem to have sprung from the pages of the Chamber of Commerce magazine. Searching in vain for the social satirist of *Babbitt* or the student of American values who created *Dodsworth*, I read it with a troubled heart. It seemed, in fact, as if the gifted parodist was playing a trick on us by engaging in self-parody. But sadly, the trick was on himself. Incredibly, Red Lewis, the friend of Debs, admirer of Darrow, and seeming convert of the young radical who had come from Dartmouth College to restore his faith, had crossed over to the side of the Babbitts and Hoover's Liberty Leaguers. And in making that crossing he had seemed to leave his entire steamer trunk of talent behind him. Red Lewis had become Fred Cornplow. The rebel had become the philistine. In retrospect that process would seem to be organic and gradual. Could he ever have known his George Babbitts and Elmer Gantrys so well if he had not been their brother under the skin? Still it seemed to me at the time that on every page of *The Prodigal Parents* I could hear echoes of Red Lewis's Battle of the Junto.

I felt sick about it. As an influencer of great men I had struck out my first time at bat. Ramon Guthrie tried to console me: This switch was characteristic of Red, an intensely erratic, blow-hot-or-cold man, full of flashing intuitions, but with no guiding philosophy to hold him on course. That's why he could be a liberal, a radical, and a reactionary on three successive days. For him the only possible -ism was intuitivism.

As if to dramatize this description (thereby adding injury to insult), Red finally did go over to inspect the marble strike as I had asked him to, only to give what I considered aid and comfort to the enemy with his statement to the *Rutland Herald* that he was not particularly impressed with the marble workers' cause. Ramon Guthrie and I managed to get our easily exacerbated author to modify this rush to judgment so as not to do further damage to the marble workers. We gathered that Red had not calmed down from his 100-proof rage when he sounded off against the strike in Rutland. It was not the strikers he was mad at. He simply lumped them impulsively with those goddamned Dartmouth brats and the Marxist manifestoes they used in place of human speech.

If this were fiction instead of fact, my narrative would come to a downbeat climax here with Lewis not only wreaking literary vengeance on the smart-ass generation that had done 'im wrong, but swearing to eat me alive if ever I climbed up his beanstalk again. The truth is somewhat less tumultuous. After the Junto fiasco I saw Lewis less often, but I still dropped in occasionally. A few days before graduation exercises I drove over to tell him the good news that Bennett Cerf, the president of Random House, on one of his flying lecture tours, had stopped off at Dartmouth long enough to pick up on my marble-strike series and had offered me a contract with a modest advance in case I "ever thought of doing a novel." I had published a couple of short stories in little magazines and was in that first happy flush of taking myself seriously as a writer. I told Red I was thinking of settling down near Dartmouth and taking a stab at my college marble-strike idea. Red thought that would be a damn-fool mistake. (That is always the way I remember him talking—profane, spontaneous, and violently opinionated.) "You come from one of the crazy American cities!" he shouted, "*Los Angeles!* What a novel there is in L.A.!" I should go home and write what I knew, the city I knew, not the marble strike that he looked on as a temporary affection or a passing phase. He hung on to that point, and a year or so later when I *was* back in Los Angeles, he wrote a pointed little essay in *Newsweek* that began: "There is in Hollywood, which is the beauty-factory or Jersey City district of Los Angeles, a young man who graduated not long ago from a New England college, and who wants to go back to the little stone-walled fields and write fiction. Well . . . if my young friend really wants to write fiction, he is deserting in Los Angeles a gold mine for which Balzac or Frank Norris or even Dickens would have given anything—except possibly, Dickens his fancy waistcoats . . ." The piece was practically a playback of my graduation-week conversation with Red Lewis, without the choice four- and five-letter words, as he walked me out to my car and presented me with an inscribed copy of *It Can't Happen Here*. "To my fellow counter-revolutionist," he had written, "even though he doesn't know it." Another five years of Party-line convulsions were to pass before I was to find myself as disillusioned and later outraged by the doctrinaire left as he had been the night he was Red-Lewis-baited.

I took maybe half of Red's literary advice, which is about all one should expect of a very young man. I finally gave up the marble-strike project and for my first novel went back to my town and some firsthand responses to the film industry I had been exposed to since childhood. But I did find it more conducive to finish that book in the stone-fenced country of Vermont.

Although I continued to see Lewis now and then, I can't remember either of us ever mentioning *The Prodigal Parents* again. Like the five forgotten novels before *Main Street,* which put him and Main Street permanently on the map, *Parents* turned out to be one of his most appalling failures. I hardly could have felt more responsible if I had written the irascible work myself.

But even sadder to tell, this book was not a brief, angry aberration but an augury. There were other novels of Red Lewis's through the 1940s, but, with the possible exception of *Kingsblood Royal,* they were put down as flabby Americana, difficult for a Lewis fan to place on the same shelf with the books our first winner of the Nobel Prize was writing in his thirties rather than his fifties. From age thirty-five to forty-five, Sinclair Lewis had performed the hat trick plus two, producing every other year a work of fiction that enhanced his reputation and lent vigor and definition to the American Novel. But by the time Red Lewis was fifty-five, he was, in the strange tradition of American letters, a burned-out old man.

Dr. Hindsight, that god of the all-knowing, has taught us that the Nobel Prize of 1930 had not been awarded to the irreverent novelist alone but to an America coming of age, to a new generation that had produced not only Lewis but Dreiser,

Anderson, Frost, Edith Wharton, Willa Cather, Hemingway, Fitzgerald, e. e. cummings, Dos Passos, and Wolfe. Red's easily ruffled feathers had been disturbed by the counterclaims in favor of Dreiser and other distinguished rivals. Even while Lewis was on his way to Stockholm to accept the mighty Prize, his critics had been trying to whittle him down as a mere super-journalist and caricaturist. And Red, who was both too arrogant and too uncertain of his own ability, had sounded the alarm to a friend as he looked down from the heights of *The Prize*; this would be the end of him: "This is fatal. I cannot live up to it."

In the early forties, when my first book, *What Makes Sammy Run?*, appeared, I'm afraid I already had begun to think of Sinclair Lewis not as a living inspiration (like the John O'Hara of *Appointment in Samarra,* or the John Steinbeck of *In Dubious Battle*) but as a relic of our literary history. This fall from grace was further emphasized by the publication of *Bethel Merriday,* a novel that seemed to confirm the creative collapse that Red himself had predicted in his rainbow year of 1930. *Bethel Merriday* was a thinly disguised portrait of a teen-age would-be actress with whom Red had been traveling on the straw-hat theater circuit, passing her off as his "niece" after the inevitable breakdown of his marriage to Dorothy Thompson.

In this period Red and I met occasionally in the office of the editor whose friendship and solicitude we now happened to share; this was the selfless Saxe Commins, who had brought Eugene O'Neill to Random House and had nursed Bill Faulkner through his agonies. He had held Red's trembling hand on many occasions when the fireball of American letters, who may be the inventor of the modern American novel, was sinking into a bewildered darkness. When Red wrote a feeble play entitled *Angela Is Twenty-Two,* embarrassingly tailored to the histrionic talents of his comely young protégée and her fifty-six-year-old protector, and insisted on touring with her in this unfortunate vehicle, I remarked to Saxe—regretfully, though perhaps with the arrogance of youth and the taste of my own early success—that Red Lewis appeared to be entering his second childhood.

Saxe Commins, an unsung St. Francis of the publishing world, long-suffering, infinitely patient, and immaculately discreet, expressed the hope that Red's lapses would prove to be only a passing phase—a bridge to a new period of productivity and maturity that would restore his friend to the pinnacle from which he had toppled.

There was to be a kind of last gasp with *Kingsblood Royal,* when Red tried to settle down to serious research in Duluth, returning in forlorn desperation to his Middle Western roots, to face into a major social problem: the failure of our white culture to accept the Negro American into the mainstream of first-class citizenship. The issue still remains at the center of our efforts to prove the validity of our democratic experiment. Red had hold of a live one here, at least another *It Can't Happen Here,* an effective propaganda novel if less than a work of art. But for all its good intentions, the focus in *Kingsblood* is so soft, the author's grip on his material inadequate to the inherent force of that material. And Red's craftsmanship seemed increasingly weary or careless. I happened to be in Commins' office going over the galleys of my second novel when the *Kingsblood* galleys came in. Saxe had pored over the manuscript with Red at his new country home in Williamstown, but he knew that the writing was still uneven and he had queried many paragraphs in red pencil on the galleys. Red had answered Saxe with a note that confirmed my fears that he was letting his creative responsibilities go by proxy. The note simply permitted Saxe to make those changes and cuts he thought judicious. Engaged writers fight like tigers over every comma.

Red seemed to know, in appointing Saxe his surrogate, that *Kingsblood Royal* would never be the novel of social protest he had hoped to achieve. The novel of political idealism, the book Red Lewis all his life had wanted to write, and for which I once had been chosen to serve as a youthful model, had wound up as a bloodless tract. The fact that it touched a nerve, carried a glittering name, and achieved bestsellerdom despite negative reviews, only etched more deeply the predicament of a failed seer who came into his sixties with nothing more to say, his talent in disarray, his familiar American bridges collapsing behind him, his health destroyed through the excesses of escape. Who would have guessed that the irascible defender of "Write America First!" would wind down in Italy as the kind of driven expatriate he had ticked off so spitefully when I first met him in Vermont?

Just twenty years after the Nobel Prize had recognized the champion of the new American novel, the wreck of Red Lewis gave up the ghost in Rome. Destroyed by fame and self-destroyed by the bitter knowledge of the premature failure of his genius, he had been dying, slowly and terribly, ever since he finished *Dodsworth* at the age of forty-three. The speech in Stockholm that had rung out like a challenge to American philistinism, that had riled American traditionalists, and that had promised so much, turned out to have been his swan song.

These days I meet young readers who groove on Kurt Vonnegut and have never read or have barely heard of Vonnegut's predecessor. Thus do youth and time devour age and achievement. More swiftly in America, I am convinced, than any place on earth. But hail and farewell, irascible, lovelorn Red Lewis, and thanks for the drinks, the hospitality, the superb mimicry, the good talk, the raucous laughter, and the fierce spirit that for one prodigious decade and a few years more blazed a path through the familiar but still unexplored social jungle of Babbittland.

II ✦ ✦ WILLIAM SAROYAN
Ease and Unease on the Flying Trapeze

"... in 1935 ... I met George Gershwin at a big party in New York and I asked him, 'How did you do it? It's the music of youth, expectation and sorrow. Can you do it again?' Gershwin tried to tell me how he had done it, and he said he didn't believe he could do it again."

—FROM *Days of Life and Death and Escape to the Moon* BY WILLIAM SAROYAN

MUCH AS WE MAY LIKE to think so, no one ever really discovers a new writer. It is something like discovering a continent. A new world is revealed through a long series of discoveries and rediscoveries, by adventurers either with no knowledge of the explorations that preceded theirs or acting on hints, whispers, rumors, and superstitions. Discovery is essentially a communal achievement, though all of us like, for the sake of simplicity and neatness, to award that big D to one particular intrepid or persistent or obsessed individual, an Eric the Red, a Columbus, a Magellan. Spiritually or psychologically, it mattered little if the Norsemen had reached the shores of North America five hundred years before the idea even popped into the heads of the oceangoing Columbus brothers. Even though he thought he had reached the outer islands of China, the Genoa-born "Admiral" of the Spanish ocean knew the joy and pride of original discovery when he stumbled upon the humble Caribbean Arawaks and mistakenly called them "Indians."

Like beauty, literary discovery is in the eye of the beholder. So when I say that I discovered William Saroyan all I mean to say is that I experienced the Columbian joy and pride of discovering him for myself. This goes back to the ancient history of the early thirties, when my bible was *Story* magazine, the monthly labor of love turned out by Whit Burnett and Martha Foley, devoted purely and entirely to perhaps the one cultural expression in which our country seems to have excelled—the short story. Quite a few of the good old writers were in *Story* but, far more important, practically all of the good new ones. Although the rewards, in terms of dollars, were negligible, as little as twenty-five dollars, acceptance in *Story* signaled one's entrance into the literary circle. It was *Story* that sponsored the

Intercollegiate Short Story Contest that triggered interest in this indoor sport all over the country (I was, for instance, inordinately proud of my honorable mention in the Intercollegiates of 1935); more to the point, it was *Story* that brought me to Bill Saroyan. It was 1934 and I was riding a Santa Fe Chief home to California from Dartmouth, reading *Story* religiously from cover to cover. In these days of dynamic technology we take it for granted that coast-to-coast travel is a matter of five jet hours, hardly time to settle in, have your two drinks, lunch, scan the magazines, snooze, unfasten seat belt, and elbow your way to the baggage chute. But those were the days of the leisurely Pullman and the time you "lost" in clickety-clacking across the continent was time found for luxuriously uninterrupted reading.

I remember being contentedly cocooned somewhere in the middle of America when there burst upon me a short-story explosion by a then-unknown young Armenian-American from Fresno, California. It was called *Seventy Thousand Assyrians*. It didn't read like Hemingway or Morley Callaghan or Daniel Cornel De Jong. That, as I knew from my own bit of undergraduate trying, took some doing in those days. It was absolutely its own voice. It was impudent, it was audacious, it was true. It dared to be not only its own content but its own form. You will never know how difficult that is to do until you try it.

In the months to come I waited and watched for more Saroyan. *Aspirin Is a Member of the NRA. The Daring Young Man on the Flying Trapeze.* They were the stories of the vigorous peasantry of the California valleys and autobiographical tales of a penniless, irrepressible country boy coming of age in the streets of San Francisco, peddling papers and a crazy love for the world. The fact that this world was hardly reciprocating the attention he was lavishing on it seemed to disturb him not at all. In a day when hope bore a Marxist, a New Deal, or a union label, Saroyan's brand of hope was individualist, woolly, and wild. His stories had a fresh way of proclaiming that the world is our oyster even if we never find a pearl. From his first entry in *Story* and gathering momentum with each subsequent contribution, I talked Saroyan wherever I went. I'm afraid I have the spirit of a crusading medicine-man. If I think I have discovered a tonic for what ails us, I love to hawk it. Often I turned visitors into a captive audience, begging them to sit still and listen while pages of this new enthusiasm were read aloud.

After reading five or six of these stories, I was curious to meet Saroyan. As I mentioned in the introduction to these reminiscences, it was still *de rigueur* in those days for writers to seek each other out. I simply went up to San Francisco, not specifically for that purpose but just to roam around that eminently roamable city, and mentioned to somebody, either another writer or a well-read bartender, that I would like to find Saroyan. Nothing could be easier. In a little while Bill Saroyan materialized, a stocky, dark-haired, carelessly dressed young man who moved, talked, and laughed with great bursts of confidence. I found him refreshingly, unabashedly, somewhat foolishly but altogether disarmingly full of himself. He was delighted but not at all surprised to hear how I had been touting his stories. They were, he said, probably the best stories that had ever been written. But he uncursed this curse with booming laughter that was infectious and let us all in on his great joke: here I am, a young, uneducated, Fresno Armenian grape-picking, hell-raising poet, an inspired moment of time who knows more about letters than all the lettered gentlemen of the world. When he said, Who is Hemingway and how can anybody possibly compare his stuff with Saroyan?, you could not fault him for enlarged ego or overconceit, for this was not adult fantasy but a rare and delicious childlike exuberance. It was Look, no hands! I'm the greatest bike rider in the whole world! Every word he put down was a holy miracle to him, the son of an immigrant Armenian vineyard worker, who could not only talk the adopted language but use these words to make beautiful American sentences!

Bill seemed to be living on his checks from *Story*, which was not unlike living on air, as I was soon to learn myself, from the joyous experience of selling them my first novelette (*Passport to Nowhere*) and then waiting nearly a year for my triumphant emolument of fifty dollars. But Bill was by his own admission the world's greatest living writer, and if ever the cliché "poor but happy" was to be dusted off and made to shine like a brand-new quarter, it was for the twenty-six-year-old Bill Saroyan, who truly flew through the thirties with the greatest of ease. The image of the quarter comes readily to mind because Bill's love affair with the world included an abiding affection for the horse rooms of San Francisco, and he happened to mention that he had been fortunate enough to find a bookie interested in the encouragement of American letters. This patron of the arts would accept bets as minimal as a fourth of a dollar, a sum that Bill was temporarily without due to the fact that *Story* paid off a good deal more slowly than the "books."

When we left him that evening to head back to L.A., my wife sneaked a dollar bill into his coat pocket because we had begun to worry whether he was deriving sufficient nourishment from the sheer joy of being alive, of living in San Francisco, of being Armenian, and outwriting Ernest Hemingway. Somewhere in one of the deep storage boxes filled with the haphazard accumulation of thirty-five years, there may still be the little note that eventually arrived from Saroyan thanking me for my largesse and bravely announcing that he had put the dollar on the nose of a horse he had been admiring. The animal, alas, had not returned his trust, but Bill sounded not in the least daunted. Not only had riches been poured down upon him in the form of fifty golden dollars from *Story* but he had been averaging at least a story a day, not one of them less than a masterpiece.

In the middle thirties my father, B.P., left Paramount, where he had been in charge of production for a decade, to open a small independent studio of his own across the street. There I heard him complaining one day about the routine, hackneyed, bloodless dialogue that was making his scripts a deadly chore to read or act. I reminded B.P. of some of the outrageously original dialogue that sparked the Saroyan stories I had cornered him into reading over the past two years. By this time the first dozen or so had been collected between hard covers under the apt title of *The Daring Young Man on the Flying Trapeze,* and with its instant success, Saroyan had gained the explosive reputation of an *enfant terrible.* But even a short-story volume as welcome as Bill's is not exactly a one-way ticket to financial independence. Bill had done his bold Armenian best to help the sales along, characteristically hawking his own wares on the ferry boats plying San Francisco Bay. But the word had come down to me through mutual friends that Bill was still short of money, possibly due to those friendly horse rooms. And so my father was encouraged, to put it gently, to wire that writing fool of an Armenian to come down to the Hollywood salt mines at what then seemed to be the munificent salary of two hundred and fifty dollars a week.

So Saroyan came down, bringing to our sunkist, overly routined dream-factory town his unruly, creative vitality, his tongue-in-cheek but effective defiance of artistic and commercial conventions, his outrageous, inimitable individuality. His sense of motion-picture construction was nil, and he hardly made a secret of his disinterest in the kind of vehicles my father had chosen. But in spite of shortcomings and misgivings, he was able to run through those routine scripts and give them a little something of his own offbeat ebullience. There was something called *A Doctor's Diary* in which the obstetrician's delivery of a baby was accompanied by a page of hackneyed sentimentality. Bill's attack on this scene was to have the doctor slap the baby and say, "Okay, baby, this is the world . . . inhale, exhale . . ." launching into one of those high-spirited Saroyanesque monologues. Coming from a doctor it was pretty strange and wild talk, but it did shake the scene out of its pedestrian mold. Some of it was even heard in the final version, and all of it was tenderly preserved for a subsequent Saroyan short story entitled, naturally, *Okay, Baby, This is the World.*

Naturally, too, Bill gravitated to our hangout at the Stanley Rose Book Store on Hollywood Boulevard just west of that other fabled artery known as Vine Street. In those pre-hip-expresso-bongo days, Stanley's was the nearest thing to a Left Bank we had out there. The back room, an art gallery of sorts, was the clubhouse for the boys who thought of themselves as artists or at least word writers rather than film hacks. There Nathanael (Pep) West, Jo Pagano, John Fante, Aben Kandel, the painter Fletcher Martin, and sometimes John O'Hara, Bill Faulkner, and half a dozen others who took themselves seriously would sit around drinking Stanley's orange wine and talking about Malraux and Mussolini and Mayer and girls and what was wrong with Hollywood and the great things we could accomplish if only we had the time.

Our host the proprietor, whose life was soon to become entwined with Bill's, was one of the damnedest patrons of the arts any of us had ever known. He came from Texas and there was size to his drinking, his cussing, his wenching, and his generosity. His love of books was deep even though he liked to insist that he never read one. He ran the best bookstore in town, catering to all the studios and carrying charge accounts with practically every famous star, director, and writer in the film community. He was untidy and unbusinesslike, rarely bothering to collect his bills and meanwhile picking up the tabs for his writer pals with a lavish hand when they went next door to their favorite restaurant-bar, Musso & Frank's. He would stake anybody he respected. On Thursday afternoons Stanley would often leave to go hunting with Pep West. Sometimes he would close the store with a sign that announced simply: Gone hunting. He would come back Monday or when he felt like it. He was one of the few free spirits in a factory town. He thought a lot of West, both as a writer and as a man. He also pushed Saroyan, who was his other closest writer friend, though Pep and Bill could not have presented more of a contrast, Pep quiet, shy, withdrawn, despising but resigned to his hack work on Westerns at Republic, but hardly ever willing to talk about what he really wanted to do or was, in odd moments, doing; Bill garrulous, audacious, boastful (but never pompous or arrogant), and often sounding like his own work, the best and the worst of it. Ask West how his book was going and he would shrug and give you a mysterious smile. Ask Saroyan and he would shout, "The story I wrote last night, in two hours and ten minutes, is the greatest thing I've ever written!" It was in a rare moment of restraint that Bill inscribed his first book to me: "From one good writer to another." As I remember Pep West, he would rather talk about shooting ducks than writing books; for Bill Saroyan the favorite indoor and outdoor sport was writing and talking about his writing. Holding forth in the back room of Stanley Rose's (Edmund Wilson was curiously accurate in thus grouping us ignobly in his *Boys in the Back Room*), Bill might have struck Pep, Fletcher, Aben, and me as pretentious if he hadn't been so innocent, so Apollonianly young, and so leavened with the spirit of the comedian. And his spirit was infectious. I found that in his presence I and the others around me talked a little louder, indulged more conceits in the earlier century's sense, and let our humor, our confidence, and our imagination range more widely.

It was in this heady atmosphere over the inevitable orange wine in the art gallery one afternoon that Bill, Stanley, and I were talking about Bill's next book. Bill seemed to be having a little trouble with Random House, which, like all publishers, was a trifle shaky about publishing successive books of short stories without sandwiching that coveted novel in between. The first collection had been a *succès d'estime* but its sale had been a respectable nine thousand—not the runaway best-seller its impact on the literary world might have suggested. In addition, there seemed to be some friction between Bill and his New York editors as to how many stories and which particular ones should be selected from his rapidly growing assortment. On the third glass of orange wine we decided to set up an impromptu publishing house and put out the book ourselves. Stanley had a small printing press on the little mezzanine balcony. He and I and a few other regulars would chip in the money. Stanley would be the publisher, I the editor, Bill would be the lead-off author for our "list." Our assets were five hundred dollars, fifteen Saroyan stories, and the sweat of my editorial brow. Could an embryo publishing house ask for more?

With a bulging portfolio of Saroyan under my arm I approached my desk with the eager pride of a young captain mounting the bridge of his first command. The original fifteen stories had burgeoned to thirty; Saroyan stories did not develop slowly like orchids, but popped up overnight like dandelions. I winnowed them carefully, squeezing them down to a tight sixteen, arranged them in what I thought would be their best order, wrote a brief introduction, set up a table of contents, and cheerfully informed Stanley Rose that we were all set to go—when in came Bill with another large envelope full of stories. Some of the new ones seemed better than the ones I had, some struck me as just so-so Saroyan, and a few seemed to me little more than unpublishable fragments. But in that ecumenical way of his, Bill loved them all and seemed unable to make any distinction between those that were truly gifted—which meant that nobody in America was doing anything better in short form just then—and those that were colorful but formless and finally expendable vamping-till-ready typewriter exercises. He was like the loving father of forty-five children, to whom the homely ones and the backward ones are just as desirable and worthy of tender care as the more beautiful and brilliant. Already we had crossed the bar from our first romantic, orange-wine dream of publishing into the everyday world of hard realities. Even though we might raise the ante by a hundred dollars or so, we had had in mind a reasonably slender volume, not the jumbo size that Bill would require if he were to publish the entire body of his proliferations. Some of them, I argued, were not stories at all but hasty little essays of questionable merit, including one on Saroyan's theory of labor value. People should work for love and not for money, Bill theorized, and even granting that he had a point—a brief, premature chirping of *The Greening of America*—I questioned whether it belonged in that always crucial second book, on which the writer of a first-effort surprise success frequently faces critics with sharpened knives.

"Besides," I insisted, "when you're writing your short stories you're on your own, unique, in your own ball park. But when you wander into the field of labor theories, status in a capitalist society, surplus value, and all the rest of it, then I think you might read some of our peers, like, well say Thorstein Veblen." At that time I navigated my little craft according to Veblen's north star and *The Theory of the Leisure Class* was my guidebook.

"No, I'd rather not read Veblen, or Engels, or Nietzsche or anybody else like that," Bill insisted, and when I pressed him for his reasons, he amplified, "Because how do I know that I won't have those same ideas myself, and if I read it somewhere else first it might keep me from writing it my own way."

With rosy visions of Bill Saroyan stumbling onto his own version of *The Theory of the Leisure Class,* or *The Engineer and the Price System,* I went back to work, shaping the material down to some twenty stories that even Bill seemed to agree were the cream of the ever-growing crop. It would cost a little more, but, after all, our original back-room purpose was to give Bill the sort of creative satisfaction the big publishers of Madison Avenue seemed to be denying him. Once more I managed the stories into what I thought was their most effective order, and once more I alerted Stanley Rose to warm up his presses when—but of course you have guessed it—in came another batch of stories. This was not quite the end of our noble adventure in attempting to launch that unexploded literary rocket, the Stanley Rose Press, but it is as good a place to stop as any. Stanley and I still loved Bill and still felt as positive as ever about his unique place in the world of the short story, but we were literally being smothered in short stories. At the incredible rate that Bill could turn them out, it was not unlike shoveling a path from your door during a raging snowstorm. Incidentally, this

book, or the even more abundant flowering of it, did emerge
from Random House a year later, still called *Inhale and Exhale,*
comprising no fewer than seventy-five stories and five hundred
pages, probably the largest single-authored, previously uncol-
lected volume of stories of all time. Saxe Commins, then the
Random House editor, had wanted to separate wheat from chaff
and size it down just as I had in its earlier form. Holding to
the best of them, he believed, would produce a fitting companion for the first book, every bit as fine as *The Daring Young
Man* . . . But Bill, as was his nature, stood by his conviction
and his seventy-five children. Although Saxe and Bill continued
to be friends there was professional tension and Bill eventually
moved on to Harcourt, Brace and other houses. What I in my
amateur way and Saxe as a long-established senior editor had
been trying to do, was impose some discipline on a talent that
was running wild. It was like trying to build a mud dam against
a river on the rampage, a fresh and fertilizing river, mind you,
but voluminously overflowing.

While Bill had been dutifully if erratically adding his fillips
to my father's scenarios, he confided to me that he was working on an ingenious scheme to free himself from even the benevolent bondage of Schulberg Studio. It was an imaginative
plan that would buy the time he needed for his own nonconformist work. There followed a typical Saroyan dream of glory.
From his two-hundred and fifty dollars a week Bill had been
saving against the day when he would amass a thousand dollars. Meanwhile, he had been studying the track very carefully.
There was a certain horse he had his eye on. He could see from
the workouts and from occasional races in which this horse
wasn't being punished to win that his candidate was being
brought along slowly but surely. When the day was right, when
both Bill and the horse were ready, he would bet the bundle.
Then, with his winnings, say five to ten grand, he would go
off to New Orleans or somewhere, dig in for a year or so, and
write more and better than he had ever written before.

I remember the day we went to the track. If what you are

about to read sounds far-fetched, charge it to my theory that some people have the faculty for acting out their dreams. So if Saroyan should sound like a character in a wildly imagined Saroyan plot, that is the way the author bounces. I walked along with Bill as he got ready to make his big move. I thought I'd take a somewhat less grandiose gamble on the same number. Our horse—I'm no longer sure of the names in this long-ago scramble—we'll call Shasta Rose. In the line to the pari-mutuel window, there was a nondescript old horse-player type in front of us who apparently overheard us discussing Bill's carefully seeded hopes for Shasta Rose. With the Scotland Yard discretion of his kind, he shook his head in a silent, almost imperceptible negation. "No?" Bill said. The mysterious stranger's answer was to sneak his index finger in the direction of his own choice on his well-penciled program—Missouri Boy. "You seem to be very confident," Bill said. The man merely nodded affirmatively, but in a way that invoked the powers of an oracle. In that moment there wasn't the slightest doubt in either of our minds that the only possible winner of the next race was Missouri Boy. Bill thanked him, very politely, followed him to the window and put his Schulberg Studio savings down on this silent benefactor's tip.

At the far turn Missouri Boy started to run over horses, and as he came into the stretch it was a one-horse race with Bill's money out in front by at least six lengths. Any moment I expected the horse to burst out singing in Bill's honor, "Way down yonder in New Orleans." Bourbon Street, here comes Saroyan, the champion writer-gambler of the age! And then, the Caliban of Hollywood Park played a lowdown juvenile-delinquent trick on Missouri Boy. Unaccountably he stumbled, shattered a foreleg, and had to be destroyed. Bill's characters frequently have been accused of an oversupply of sweetness and light, but I shall always remember how his reaction to this costly little tragedy out-Saroyaned the most forebearing of Saroyan's "people with the light coming out of them." Turning away from the scene of the crime we encountered the crestfallen oracle who had pitched us onto Missouri Boy. I'm sorry, the man said. Shasta Rose, far back in the place position, had gone on to win the race, and Bill, instead of being wiped out, would have taken home around seventy-five hundred dollars on his original pick. But, in the poetic Saroyan style that is too good for this world, he told the sorry tipster, "Don't feel bad. I should be grateful to you for trying to help me. Missouri Boy was the horse to bet. Only God could have known he was going to break his leg. So thank you anyway."

On the way back to town I asked Bill what he was going to do now. "Go back to San Francisco," he said. But now, I argued, he needed that job with my father more than ever. And then in three months from now . . . Bill stopped me with a shake of his head. "No, my plan has failed," he decided with his own quixotic logic. "I have to go back to San Francisco and start all over again."

More than any other writer I have known, Bill Saroyan lived, wrote, and acted from the top of his emotions. He had this lovely, naïve, ridiculous, and enviable faith in his own spontaneity. There was, for instance, an attractive young lady in a Beverly Hills bookstore who was much taken with Bill, a bull-in-china-shop ladies' man with his strongly sculptured head, dark hair, soulful eyes, forceful fieldworker's physique, and unpredictable gusto. He and the young bookstore lady had been going together long enough to encourage her to the conviction that this was more than a casual relationship. One morning, in the small hours, Bill suddenly called her, announced that he was lonely, and asked her to get herself over to his place immediately. She lectured him nicely. "Bill, dear, you know I'm very, very fond of you but you just can't call a girl up in the middle of the night and tell her to come right over as if she were just a—" To which Bill countered innocently, "Okay, in that case, what's your sister doing?"

Bill's attitude toward politics was equally his own. A huge mass meeting to welcome Malraux was being held in downtown Los Angeles in support of the Spanish Loyalists, and I urged

Bill to come with me. His work was devoted to the pure in heart, but more or less in a vacuum, I argued. In Spain the innocent majority was beset by Franco's Falange, actively abetted by Mussolini and Hitler. Bill might learn something from Malraux and the spirit of the meeting. So we went and we listened and Malraux was his lean, intense, effective, apocalyptic self and the antifascist multitude responded with emotional if vicarious *"No pasarans!"* With one eye on Malraux and the other on Saroyan, I felt confident that I was leading the latter ever so subtly to our cause. But on the drive back to Hollywood Bill was still his own sweet apolitical self. "I'm for the people over there defending themselves against Franco," Bill said, "but I'm also for the poor peons trying to keep alive in Franco's army. There are plenty of those, too. How can you be on one side or the other when the people are on both sides?" We argued that one a long time, to a draw.

This was the same William Saroyan who—while the Hollywood Communists hid under secret party names and prudently refused to come out openly for Earl Browder in the presidential campaign—freely lent his name to a Browder-for-President committee. There were some raised Hedda-Hopperish eyebrows but I and Bill's other good friends understood. Bill had no use for Communism and vice versa. In his heart Bill was an anarchistic gambling-manchild-writer. Coming out publicly for Browder while avoiding the catch-all Popular Front causes to which nine out of every ten American writers were then dedicated was simply Bill's way of playing the Goof, the dewy-eyed forerunner of the hipster, a premature laughing-boy disaffiliator. Today, the nonstructured revolutionaries express rebellion by coming out against Nixon, Humphrey, clipped hedges, clean sneakers, syntax, nine-to-five jobs, and the hydrogen bomb. Bill Saroyan, equally antisquare but basically more sentimental and more (or is it the same thing?) positive, had to come out for something that season, so why not the homey Kansas Communist Earl Browder?

But let us not belabor. For Saroyan and Politics is not a

subject; at its best, a brief if telltale footnote to this informal glance at his life and his time.

During the later thirties, when I was nine-to-fiveing in the Hollywood vineyards and writing short stories nights or weekends, I kept in touch with Bill. In the summer of 1938, for his thirtieth birthday, I went up to San Francisco not so much to celebrate as to commiserate with him. I have always found writers even more sensitive than women to the milestones of age. Writers in their twenties enjoy some of the latitude permitted thoroughbred two-year-olds. If they are unpredictable and skittish in the starting gate, if they have not learned how to move between horses or even to run in a straight line, if they do not yet know how to put their talent for speed or endurance under the rein of discipline and form, they are forgiven, encouraged, and loved for the bright promise screened but not hidden by their immaturity. To gallop on with our metaphor, if not ride it to death, it is not demanded of a prize two-year-old that he run the full Belmont distance. And the same sort of allowances are enjoyed by our writers under thirty. Gather ye rosebuds while ye may, o highly praised young bard, for the world that pressed you to its bosom at twenty-nine may unceremoniously toss you out on your ear for writing the same stuff at thirty-one. Whether or not this is objectively true, it seems to hold a terrible, subjective truth for all the writers to whom I have been exposed.

To his dying day, John O'Hara never forgave the critic who greeted *Butterfield 8,* the novel with which he followed the stunning *Appointment in Samarra,* with the witticynicism "Disappointment in O'Hara." It does seem as if some critics feel an irresistible urge to make amends for the blessings they have bestowed. With *Waiting for Lefty* and *Awake and Sing,* Odets was hailed as *the* playwright of the thirties but soon came the irresistible whiplash, "Odets, where is thy sting?" Similarly was the young Irwin Shaw carried triumphantly from the field on the critics' shoulders after *Bury the Dead* but these same gods of the weathervane had hardly hoisted him skyward when they were abruptly disengaging themselves and dropping him back into the mud. In vain did Mr. Shaw, in introductions to later plays, cry out against the abuse he reaped for his prodigious sowing. He was virtually driven from the theater as a thirty-five-year-old failure. We seem to have a bull market in young writers, we delight in overpricing them and then selling them short and even pushing them off the board. American writers, from Melville to Mailer, if they are to survive the success-failure syndrome, need, as covering for their vulnerable hearts, extremely tough hides.

Bill Saroyan, heretofore the most absurdly confident young writer I had ever met, was singing the familiar writers' blues on that Birthday of the Great Divide between ages twenty-nine and thirty. *What shall I do now that I'm not a Young Writer any more?* For the first time in the five years I had known him, I found him self-critical, realistically appraising his work according to the more demanding standards he expected of his thirties. "I've got to go forward," Bill was saying somewhere along the Embarcadero. "A few more collections like the ones I've been turning out and they'll start to say that Saroyan is a flash in the pan. A writer of good if rather formless sketches, just a lot of vignettes, that's what they'll say. Good early stuff but no follow-through, that's what they'll start accusing me of."

A group of chums around the table were amazed. Why, this didn't even sound like our Saroyan who had been shouting into the wind not so long ago, Who is this fella Hemingway? The tables were literally reversed now and we heard ourselves trying to ease Bill's anxieties by telling him that there was no law making every writer a novelist or a playwright. A man could be a good vignettist in this world and make that important, too.

But this time it was not enough for Bill to be the Saroyan that had enchanted him and other admirers through the haphazardly productive years of his youth. He would have to leave the little stories behind and produce something that would mark a dramatic departure, an announcement of his new maturity.

And then in the early hours, as we roamed his San Francisco, in some mysterious, healing, healthy way he began to take heart. He had already taken a small plunge into the deep new pool of the thirties by writing a moody, dreamlike one-act play, *My Heart's in the Highlands*. Now, he said, he would plunge deeper by writing a full-length play.

Except for college efforts I had never written a play, but youth is a heady wine and I did not hesitate to explain the theory and practice of playwriting to Saroyan. After all, I had written some film scripts and I had made a close study of John Howard Lawson's standard text on the subject and was able to hold forth for a considerable time on the inexorable laws of dramatic construction and the nature and meaning of the obligatory scene. You just can't sit down in the first flush of excitement and dash off a three-act play, I explained. If you study any successful play, from the tragedies of O'Neill to the comedies of Kaufman and Hart, you will find a strong, developed sense of form, I explained. The opening act must set up the characters and their problems and tensions that will be extended to the near-breaking point in the second act and then played out and paid off at the final curtain. I remember feeling that I was explaining it very well: how each scene must build and mount to a subclimax and the series of scenes culminate in a climax that is as inevitable as it is surprising, a moment of revelation that brings down the final curtain.

Bill laughed and waved away my wisdoms. "I don't know about all that stuff," he said. "Hemingway broke a lot of the rules when he put his first stories down and there were people who tried to tell me that mine weren't stories until they began to get the idea that I had found a new way of telling a story. So why can't I do the same thing in the theater?"

Because, I reasoned, you only have to hold the audience for twenty minutes on a short story and you can do that with mood or a fresh character sketch. But once you presume to hold them in the theater for two-and-a-half hours, you have to know what you are doing from the first line to the last, you have to be an architect as well as a quick-sketch artist.

"Budd, you do it your way; I'll do it my way," Bill said, cheerfully. "I'll make my own rules. I won't worry about this three-act-play business. Maybe it will be a one-act play three hours long. Maybe I'll have five acts, or seven. I'll just bring down the curtain when I'm finished, or whenever I feel like it. Or maybe I won't even have a curtain. I'll just let it play, the way I did my stories, only longer, and, I hope, better."

Well, we talked into the dawn, but that was the nub of it. I left Bill with the sorry feeling that he had flunked out of the Schulberg School of Dramatic Art. What a pity it was, it seemed to me, that his promising career as a writer of original short fiction was reaching so premature an end.

Early that fall, having gone East from Hollywood to devote myself to fiction, I was working on my first novel in Vermont when Bill called me from Boston. His voice was full of the old Look-Ma-I'm-writin'!-Okay-world-this-is-Saroyan! He had written the birthday play. He had indeed celebrated thirty triumphant years upon this earth by writing his first full-length play. Even Bill was unable to describe just how great the play was. I would have to hurry down to Boston and see it for myself.

In Boston I watched with wonder as *The Time of Your Life* unfolded with grace and humor and warmth and the miracle of seemingly inadvertent dramatic unity. There was Bill's San Francisco waterfront honky-tonk, not the real, miserable joint itself, but Bill's captivating, fairy-tale conception of it, filled with the lonely and beautifully pure-of-heart people that Bill believed in. Maybe to you these are nothing but lowly and undistinguished people, Bill's play said to us, with its own wacky eloquence, but look again and you will discover that the lady who seems just a two-dollar whore to the vulgar-minded has beauty and greatness and immortality in her. And the sad unemployed comedian who feels the world needs his laughter is a performing genius if we will only see him that way. And the big, good-natured American goof who falls foolishly in love with the lady who plies her trade on the outside while living a life of considerable grandeur on the inside, don't laugh at the goof because he is really you and in the time of his life he is living fully and even wisely for being able to penetrate the ugly rind of flesh and matter to the spiritual core ever-loving and incorruptible.

That's what the man wrote, and wrote so mysteriously well that Saroyan the short-story writer in his twenties was now eclipsed by the new playwright who made this play as if he had been born to the mastery of theater magic.

When the lights came on I hugged Bill (those being the days before the gay epidemic, when men could express their feelings physically without fear of being misunderstood) and told him the play was even more than he had promised on that stock-taking birthday night in San Francisco. It played, it worked, it sang, I said; it was practically perfect. *Practically,* said Bill from the top of his mountain, what was wrong with it?

Only in the very last minute did I think it faltered, I said, when the garrulous old Western braggart, Kit Carson, shoots Blick, the vice squad agent, the one hateful and hating character in the play, who must enforce morality because he is the incarnation of evil. It had seemed to me that none of the figures in the play was capable of sufficient reality to press the actual trigger of an actual gun and put an actual bullet through the head of an actual man. It seemed to me too violent an ending for so fragile a play. I could imagine Kit Carson swaggering back into the little saloon and merely boasting that he had shot the man, giving the clientele momentary relief from Blick's vicious invasion of their dreams, while the audience knows that there is no end to the Blicks, at least not in our foreseeable world.

"Great idea, you're right, we'll change it," said Bill, "let's go up and tell them!" I found myself swept through a door that led onto the stage behind the curtain. I had never been on the stage of a professional theater before. There was the great Eddie Dowling, both star and director of the play, conferring with the equally legendary brass of the Theatre Guild, Theresa Helburn and Lawrence Langner. "I think this kid has a great idea!" Bill ran up to them. I saw the way they looked at each other in pain. "Go ahead, tell 'em," Bill said happily. Suddenly I was gripped with something worse than stage fright. This was no longer the back room of Stanley Rose's Book Store, where we could bat the bull around and get excited by each other's flash ideas over a pitcher of orange wine. As I began stammering my way through my reluctant, callow, ridiculous, unwanted revision of their play, talking into the stony faces of strangers, I think I realized for the first time that this was the big time, that Bill had not only written a crazy and wonderful play that had special meaning for me, but had now moved on to partnership with famous professionals of the theater who were getting his play ready for the great night in New York and who thought he must be daft to drag in off the street and into a crucial conference an adolescent West Coast crony. Somehow, with a dry throat, I got to the end of my now meaningless bit of advice. Again they gave each other that terrible look, and without even glancing at me they said, "Bill, can we see you over here for a minute," and walked off in a body. This marked the end of my career with the Theatre Guild, as it marked Bill's beginning. I doubt if there was a more auspicious beginning in the history of the Broadway theater.

Two weeks later *The Time of Your Life* was a roaring success, hailed by the critics as an inspired adventure in the American theater and loved by audiences, who laughed at its sad jokes and found solace in its triumph of the good little people over the bad little agent of vice. Across the ocean dark powers were blitzkrieging humanity and the real Blick of the world was a Himmler whose genius for evil would eventually create a poisoned atmosphere in which it would be increasingly difficult for Bill's tender grapes to flourish. But this is hindsight. In that fool's-gold peaceful October of 1939, William Saroyan had grabbed the gold ring that only America holds forth to its artists. The daring young man was up above the world so high like a playwright in the sky. Nothing in the world bursts upon one so galvanically and blindingly as success in America and in that particular autumn in New York—despite *The Little Foxes, The Man Who Came to Dinner,* and *Life with Father,* not to mention that sensitive sleeper, *Morning's at Seven*—the playwright of the hour, like Odets five years earlier, like Tennessee Williams and Arthur Miller a decade later, was our Fresno Kid, Willie Saroyan. He was the pet of George Jean Nathan, he was the American O'Casey, and the royalties of a hit Broadway show exploded his economy. He was gazed upon by the interested eyes of the sleek young ladies of New York when he entered the public privacy of "21," and his droll observations on life and love and letters decorated the dottings of the syndicated columnists. Leonard Lyons bearded him in his Den and told a marveling world how Bill could lock himself up in a hotel room in the Great Northern and bang out a whole play in five breathless days. Peace, it's wonderful, Bill was calling to his own true-love vision of America—Love, here is my hat!

With that golden ring on the merry-go-round, Bill Saroyan had been given a free ride on everything that was swinging and whipping in the whole amusement park and I watched him, in fact cheered him on, as he rode the front seat of the first car of the roller coaster. I think that only American writers are privileged to ride that perilous catbird seat. I hope I am not saying that Bill was spoiled by success. That is true, but also too easy and therefore a cliché untruth. Yes, I remember being troubled by standing in the men's room with Bill at, yes, "21," and his talking in his good young way of the San Francisco days when he was the greatest writer in the world, but this time instead of it being a juicy Saroyan horse-laugh at the literary world, he had a review from George Jean Nathan in his pocket, and I think from Brooks Atkinson, too. You see what I mean, it wasn't that Bill had changed. But Bill's world had changed, while Bill was still the same old Saroyan, and that is admirable the way Chauvin was admirable, while his name with an -ism on the end became an epithet. It was even more true when Bill —over the damnedest collection of writers possibly ever to present plays in one year: Anderson, Sherwood, Kingsley, Lindsay and Crouse, Thurber and Elliott Nugent, Sam Raphaelson, Clare Boothe, and Paul Osborne, an all-star Broadway Olympic team—was awarded the Pulitzer Prize. And for reasons that were not showboat but perfectly sound no-foundation-all-the-way-down-the-line Saroyan reasons, he refused to accept the Prize. Saroyan was made and had it made in every possible direction.

Maybe it didn't seem so to him, or to me, watching him at the time, but the great American roller coaster was plunging faster. There were not only more Saroyan plays (see the Lyons Den for fascinating details) but a Saroyan Theater, no, not on the Embarcadero or in the little hills of Hollywood, but on Broadway, with Saroyan writing, and producing and directing and publicizing Saroyan. If the last participle sounds malicious, blame it on the turning of the wheel. The *Story* magazine Saroyan preferring Saroyan to Hemingway was charming because he spoke, to paraphrase somebody, from the authority of the undiscovered. Once discovered, or having discovered one's self, one must, alas, speak more carefully.

From a rear seat in the roller coaster (actually a side seat on a streetcar out to San Francisco's Seal Rock) I watched Bill coach young novelist John Fante on how to launch a successful play on Broadway. John was, like Bill, a small-town California writer of originality and merit who had written *Wait Until Spring, Bandini,* and a group of tender short stories. John, an Italian who looked like an Irishman, and who would have looked like a longshoreman if he wasn't such a short shoreman, told Bill, on the way out, that he was thinking of writing a play.

"I'll tell you who to send it to," said Bill, "but don't let them have it more than four weeks, otherwise they'll sit on it for a year and—" "I'll tell them two weeks and that's it!" said John. "And don't let them push you around on the casting," said Bill. "After all, you are the author, who knows better than you how to—" "I'll send them exactly the cast I want to have for the show," said John. "And the director can ruin you," said Bill. "They talk theater and think they know theater, but after all who can direct my plays better than—" "I'll tell 'em they've got two weeks and if they don't like my cast and my direction, fuck 'em!" said John, laughing, and pulling Bill's leg but also meaning every word of it. So it went, joyously, and I must say I admired them, all the way out to Seal Rock and back again. The fact that John Fante never burst onto Broadway, and that Bill never had a play included in the ten best plays of any subsequent season is probably purely coincidental. Anyway, it was one hell of a streetcar ride, with Bill, now the King of New York, instructing the engaging crown prince John on the short cuts to fame, fortune, and integrity on the Great White Way.

The Ferris wheel swung back to Hollywood again, only this time it wasn't $250 per week at the little Schulberg Studio but the big six-figure money for *The Human Comedy,* not Balzac's but Saroyan's, a briefer, kindlier study of mankind as seen through the enchanted eyes of a Western Union messenger boy. It was rather a darling little book, a Book of the Month, I'm pretty sure, a little treacly for my taste but still several cuts above the ordinary film. Bill, the iconoclast, found himself the favorite of M-G-M's last tycoon, L. B. Mayer, who had built his empire on a platform of big stars in safe stories complete with happy endings and songs you can whistle to. The height of his esthetic ambition was the Andy Hardy series, and in an odd way *The Human Comedy,* for all its nice Saroyanesque touches, was a glorified Andy Hardy. I went out to M-G-M to see Bill one day, partly because it was difficult not to feel affection for him and partly to see how my old twenty-five-dollar-a-story freewheeler was taking his new-found riches and his Hollywood preeminence. Well, Bill was taking it in stride, but a giant stride. He had Stanley Rose with him as his agent and Stanley, with his ruddy Texas face a little more rutted with whiskey, told me that Bill had stood up nobly, insisting that his pal receive 10 percent of Bill's income from the studio, which was adding up to twenty thousand dollars for Stanley's end alone. It was Bill's way of writing off the generous endowment of the bookstore days, and Stanley was never to have it so good again. They were a sight, those two strays from the honkytonks, swinging their weight around the stately halls of Metro, calling the imperious L.B. "Louie," and twisting him around with a flamboyance that none of the movie greats had ever dared display.

Love came to Bill in the form of a sexy, saucy, wealthy, witty girl by the name of Carol Marcus, a washing-machine heiress who could paint and write poetry and in the time of her life live it up to Bill's standards and perhaps beyond. I remember dining with them one night at Romanoff's. Forty-two, I think it was, and thinking how well paired they were, full of juice and hope and a fine low style. At that moment it seemed to me that Bill was close to the Everything summit most young writers only dream of scaling. He had stuck in his thumb and pulled out a plum, Miss Marcus, and he had George Jean Nathan, and he had L. B. Mayer and he had the rejected Pulitzer Prize and he had Harcourt, Brace and Leonard Lyons and Broadway waiting for his next, his next . . .

Then war came to Bill. Bill had a tough war. I don't mean Mauldin mud-in-the-face tough. Bill believed in his Christian or fairy-tale world of good people on all sides, just as he had sighed that sweet and futile hope at that mass meeting for Malraux I dragged him to during the Spanish Civil War. A war is a critical condition, like a key woman or even more so, to a writer. A writer can hate war like Dos Passos. A writer can be hurt by war like Hemingway. A writer can laugh a sardonic ha-ha at the absurdity of war, as e. e. cummings did. In World War II Irwin Shaw embraced the war partly as conscious Jew, partly as conscious writer on the prowl for material. With a tougher mind, self-consciously nonconformist Norman Mailer was eager to have at the war with a sharp left and a straight right like the brilliant old-time Jewish lightweights. And Jimmy Jones, the banger from Illinois, went into the bloodpit without too much style, a game, willing boy who knew the old Army game and came out victorious like a battered Battling Nelson. Bill wasn't able to assume any of these stances, couldn't write for it, couldn't write against it, couldn't write in it. I always thought of Bill Saroyan as a conscientious objector in uniform.

One day in New York in 1943 three valiant servicemen—Saroyan, Shaw, and Schulberg—were having lunch together at Manny Wolf's. Bill was, I think, a private in the Army, stationed at the Signal Corps film studio at Astoria. Irwin was, if memory serves, a warrant officer eager to go overseas to experience the war and to gather material for his eventual *The Young Lions*. I was, of all things, an ensign in the Navy, not exactly winning the war single-handed in the O.S.S. We talked shop, short stories, novels, and it was all pretty good food and pretty good talk, but saddened for me by Bill's description of the documentary script he was struggling with, an instructional film on how to load a boxcar. It was laced with the funny-malicious stories of retarded executive officers that reminded me of the stories we used to tell about our producers at the writers' table in the studio commissary to salve our uneasy consciences. Irwin and I commiserated with him, urged him to try to find something better, and he shrugged and said loudly, "We don't belong in this thing at all." He didn't mean the United States, he meant Saroyan, Schulberg, and Shaw, downing our oversupply of calories at Manny Wolf's. "After all, we're not soldiers, we're artists; artists don't belong to any side of war." Irwin and I, conspicuous in our uniforms, undoubtedly two of the three oddest fighting men to be found at that moment on Third Avenue, stole glances around our shoulders to see how the other tables were taking this announcement. I didn't agree with Bill, but I think I knew how he felt. It wasn't simply that he was an artist but that his scheme of things—I mean his philosophical scheme—no longer applied to a world that had to fight not the insignificant Blick but the Wehrmacht and the Luftwaffe and the Waffen-S.S. if ever it was to live out the time of its life. No, it wasn't Bill's war. And perhaps the troubles to come issued from the melancholy fact that the world that was to emerge from that war was no longer Bill's kind of world.

I ran into Bill once or twice in London during the war, where I had the feeling that he was waiting it out, positioned somewhat like heavyweight contender Billy Conn, marking time until the mess blew over and he could get back to what he had been doing so effectively in prewar days.

After the war I settled down to writing on a farm in Pennsylvania and didn't see Bill for a number of years. I kept up with him mostly through Leonard Lyons' column and through seeing an occasional play of his at colleges and little theaters. *Jim Dandy, Across the Board on Tomorrow Morning, The Beautiful People, Hello, Out There.* There were still those refreshing departures from the tired, three-wall, naturalistic theater, and each one of them was welcome to my eye and ear. But none of them seemed able to go the distance. The single line that the Arab in *The Time of Your Life* kept repeating: "No foundation. All the way down the line," became an alarmingly cryptic summary of the Saroyan theater. I don't think it was just a matter of luck on the first one and a continuing failure in technique. I think it had more to do with the fact that the postwar years were stripped of illusion, were tough and frightening, while Bill's characters and themes still bathed and wallowed and were suffused in illusion. There was a need for harder, bolder, more violent or more profound voices—Miller to remind us of social evils, and Williams as obsessed with his fables of men's vice as Bill had been inspired by their goodness. And Camus stubbornly walking the minefields of existentialism toward a new and deeper concept of dignity of man, beyond Saroyan's rosy optimism, beyond Williams' little-boy-lost pessimism, where—beyond their extremes of romanticism—he saw man groping in the dark "toward the yet invisible places where the gates will open."

Some years ago I heard that Bill was in New York and called him to say hello and wish him well. We went to a nightclub together. There were some marvelous acts on the floor, including Lena Horne, and I felt that Bill was trying to rise to the occasion with that incomparable zest for living he exuded in the earlier California days. But, through no fault of his own, there were a couple of strikes on him. In some ways, under the large curling dark mustache he had cultivated, I felt he was withdrawing into the dark brooding world of his Armenian ancestors, the people who had been trampled and kicked and starved and treated like dogs in all the wars reaching back into the dim past where history trails off into legend. Bill's marriage was smashed, under circumstances that cut to the heart of a man, and, like the good peasant father he was, he sorely missed his son Aram. Bill's money, which, as a genuine artist-gambler, he had never taken too seriously, was gone to the green tables and the horses on which he had lavished sums of Zanuckian proportions, was gone to human generosity of which he had a great store, was gone to the government, which was taxing him prodigiously (unfairly, most of us writers and fighters think) for his mighty jackpots in days past. The Broadway theater that had embraced him as its new god had moved on, in its inexorable, wise, and fickle way, to other gods. I am accustomed to seeing my friends made sad and troubled, but Bill's depression struck me with extra force. Irreverently a line from that poem we had to learn in high-school English popped to mind: *Thou wast not meant for death, immortal Bird!* I suppose what I meant was that Bill Saroyan, our high-flying yes-is-for-a-very-young-man of our first meetings fifteen years earlier, was never meant for broken marriage or jealousy or homelessness or sonlessness or mounting tax debts or cold wars or hot wars or the illusionless shadows of the Bomb.

This may sound crazy, but all this just shouldna happened to Bill Saroyan. To the rest of us, yes, because somehow, being in many ways lesser than Bill, we were better adapted to breathing the poisons.

Some years later, though I hadn't seen Bill again, I found myself thinking of him once more because the clock that refuses to stop ticking us away had swung around to 1958 and Bill's fiftieth year. Was there some breakthrough he could achieve across this barrier which could compare with that bold time of his life at thirty? He was leaving America, he announced just about then, because he owed the government so much money that he could only recoup by working in Europe. He was off to Yugoslavia to write, direct, and produce a motion picture. Then, from Yugoslavia, came word that Bill had been forced to move on, because he was unable to find the creative freedom there without which he could not function with integrity.

Now I followed his odyssey loyally and sympathetically through the dot-dot-dot items of the faithful Leonard Lyons. He is in Paris doing a movie for Darryl F. Zanuck . . . He is in New York to place his own indelible stamp on the Ali-Frazier affair . . . Or he is in London assembling a play according to his own impish fashion by first selecting the cast and placing them upon the stage and then writing down his direction of their improvisations—well, something like that. I understand the critics rebelled. But Bill is dented but not daunted. He will write a play for each European capital. On to Vienna . . . When he was at the height of his Broadway success, he is quoted as saying ruefully, all the lovely young ladies used to look his way. Now, when he passes, only an occasional middle-aged librarian raises her head.

What's the trouble? Is it the darkening social climate? Is it the ravages of success too much too soon, wrenching him from the old haunts and the people he knows best? Is it personal trouble, money trouble, or Scott Fitzgerald's old fear that there are no second acts in American lives? Was it that Bill Saroyan and his work needed to be dewy-eyed innocent and forever young?

As he pumps into his sixties, Bill Saroyan is still a daring young man on a trapeze that doesn't swing quite so close to the top of the tent. But I, who remember him with laughter, affection, and admiration, still hope to look up one day and catch sight of him swinging higher and higher until he rips right up through the top of the tent and on out of the circus grounds into the hard world of wars, taxes, infidelities, race hatreds, and population explosions of human beings mortally flawed who wait to be served by a talent and a promise finally tempered in the heat of the goddamnedest bonfire of all mantime. To these eyes peering down the shaft of five decades, it is too late for whimsy or simple faith because, for all our moon walks and Mars munchings, we still haven't got the slightest idea of how to put that fire out.

And yet, if one puts one's ear to the ground, he may hear the sound of Saroyan's footsteps, still distant, but approaching in our direction. When *The Time of Your Life* was revived in New York's Lincoln Center, most reviewers were pleasantly surprised to find that the play still retained its original flavor, its unabashed innocence, its Blakelike faith. And then the sexagenarian Saroyan was interviewed in New York and what he had to say seemed to attract more attention than it had in the years when his star seemed to be hiding behind the mushroom cloud.

In his First Season of Success, what he had to offer was a refreshing contrast to the Angries (including this one) singing of the Final Conflict and putting down the rulers of a way of life we hoped to bury. Rather than curse the darkness, he offered to share his candlelight of simple faith.

But the next generation had had little patience with his kind of goodness. The world was too cold for the warm, simple heart of the poet. Only the Beats, trailblazing and mindblowing their way for the hips, the flower kids, and the children of the counterculture, only the howling Kerowacks could hit the road, hit

the booze, hit the grass, set fire to their visions, and turn the
game around violently enough to make a dent on the (Lord
Lord remember them!) Silent Generation. The Desolation
Angels, way out ahead of their time, took over San Francisco
from Bill Saroyan. Ten years after the Daring Young Man it
was Kerouac and Ginsberg and Corso, McClure and Ferlinghetti, who made the music at the parties. But today we may
begin to relate Saroyan to the prevailing current, what I would
call "a revolution without bones," our revolution of irreverent
posters and buttons, of neo-rock and neo-folk, the unstructured
revolution in its uniform of genuinely or artificially impover-
ished jeans, faded ex-Army shirts, fringed over-the-shoulder
suede Indian bags, hip chains of fool's gold, peace medallions,
and meadow bells. Protesting against war in Indochina, con-
tamination of our air and water, straights and square jobs,
formal marriage, formal education, formal *anything,* the generation that's into Consciousness III dreams of *The Greening of
America* when love will replace law-'n'-order, and mystery and
simplified self-sufficiency will save us from technocratic stran-
gulation in the name of an inexorable Progress. I relate Saroyan
to the soft-boned revolution my daughter Vicky feels she is
part of by moving out and away from the old competitive society to tribal acres in the wilds of Idaho where material appe-
tites are to be reduced to a Thoreauvian minimum while inner
values are nourished, where nothing is eaten or used that will
corrupt, where a family in commune with other cooperative
families may rediscover and hopefully reestablish the true
values of a society from the inside out, rather than from the
outside in as we of the reform and left-political generation have
tried (and largely failed) to achieve.

The Making of a Counter Culture (which impresses me as
a less gaseous, or overgeneralized, book than our recent Number One, *The Greening of America*) concludes with George
Fox's call to "stand still in the light," suggesting that not through
action but through this stillness can men be persuaded to "give
up a way of life they inwardly loathe but which misplaced pride

goads them to defend under aggressive pressure to the very death—their death and ours." Or, as *Counter Culture* quotes Chuang-tzu, "A political end sought by no political means . . ."

This is the "antirevolution" revolution of *The Greening* "that hopes to make visible the submerged magic of the earth and bring closer that culture in which power, knowledge, achievement recede before the great purpose of life. Which is, as an old Pawnee shaman taught: 'to approach with song every object we meet.' "

If this idyllic condition of Consciousness III is achieved through nonviolence—a big and improbable "if" in this dissenter's view—then indeed will the footsteps of William Saroyan grow louder again. If innocence, kindness, and the joy of being alive overcome war, racism, and the territorial imperative, then will the works of William Saroyan come once more into their own. Consciousness III embracing Saroyan III. For the Third Season would be The Time of His Life, when his audience is as young, as apolitical, as simplistic, and as nonorganizationally and purely religious as is Saroyan, whose genius or whose folly it has been to approach with song every object he meets. "My Heart's in the Highlands," Bill Saroyan was forever singing, and if the heart of the Republic could sing along with him, then the Saroyan fame of thirty years ago will swing upward again, sweeping into that Fourth Season of Success that breathes new life into one's reputation on the far side of paradise.

But if that heart is broken and divided in the hard, dark struggle between haves and have-nots, or wills and will-nots, if it is not joyous communalism but bitter, final Armageddon, then Bill Saroyan's reputation, so richly deserved, may be swept away. A repressive history, sadly unable to cry out "Love, Here Is My Hat!" would reduce Saroyan to the asterisks reserved for minor poets. Thus is fame at the mercy of the winds of time, destroying one career, eroding another, and filling the sails of a third. If to every writer there is a season, Bill Saroyan had a lovely spring the first time around. Now that he is 30 x 2 he could be due for another, if only the young shepherds of the counterculture prevail. Let us hope so, for the sake of the loving young man on the flying trapeze who had and who still heroically maintains the courage of his innocence.*

* In his recent book of musings, a touching and tender thing called *Days of Life and Death and Escape to the Moon,* Saroyan reflects on the plight of the aging writer who knows "he can't do what he used to do," and counsels philosophical acceptance of his fate, the flagging of his "genius, inexhaustible energy and imagination, his capacity to work as if he were more than one man. . . ." An older, less exuberant, but still questing Saroyan rediscovers his immortality in the joy of survival, of seeing the first light of morning, of walking the streets that one loves. A poignant rather than acrobatic Bill Saroyan gently protests but does not resist the seasonal winds of success that have blown him to and fro.

This is admirable and even quietly heroic. But why should a writer who is only sixty years old have to feel that the sensible thing "is not to blow his brains out but to take it slow and easy, not feeling obliged to be a kind of hero of the world, and not being miserable about the fact that he has changed, as all things must change"? Bill Saroyan has always been an intensely *American*-Armenian, for only American artists seem to suffer this kind of resignation so early in the game.

III ⋄⋄ OLD SCOTT
The Myth, the Masque, the Man

". . . that first wild wind of success and the delicious mist it brings with it . . . a short and precious time—for when the mist rises in a few weeks, or a few months, one finds that the very best is over."

> —F. SCOTT FITZGERALD, *Early Success, Esquire*, 1937. HIS REQUIEM FOR HIS FIRST SEASON OF SUCCESS WITH *This Side of Paradise*, WHEN HE WAS THE ARROW-COLLAR *Wunderkind* OF 1920

". . . the succeeding period of desolation and of the necessity of going on . . . I could no longer fulfill the obligations that life had set for me or that I had set for myself . . . where was the leak through which, unknown to myself, my enthusiasm and my vitality had been steadily and prematurely trickling away . . . ?"

> —FROM *Pasting It Together, Esquire*, 1936

ALTHOUGH I KNEW F. Scott Fitzgerald for a relatively short time, over the last two years of his life, I felt I knew him well. Our fevered service as collaborating screenwriters on location at Dartmouth College to concoct a movie around the Winter Carnival was an ordeal that could only split us out forever or bring us closer together than a famous if neglected forty-three-year-old author and a twenty-five-year-old apprentice ever could have been on such short acquaintance. Our journey, if it achieved nothing more, did accomplish the latter, and since the half-true, half-imagined *Disenchanted* ended with its hero's death at the end of the Carnival while my friendship with Fitzgerald continued through the ensuing twenty-two months of his life, it is my memory of him in the post-Carnival period that I have thought most about but have never committed to a book of nonfiction in the thirty years he's been gone. I do this now not to blow my own little vicarious horn as a friend of the great or as a subcourier allowed to approach the throne but because I believe every one of us with firsthand impressions of Scott Fitzgerald—the black, the white, the gray, and the golden—has an obligation to share them.

Among some of his celebrated friends and relatives, there is a wish to draw a discreet curtain over Fitzgerald's memory. "I hope your play is a miserable failure," Fitzgerald's sister-in-law wrote me on the eve of the Broadway opening of *The Disenchanted*. And there followed the humanly understandable but professionally unrealistic plea to let sleeping bones rest. Fitzgerald was not worth all this attention, the angry note contended, recalling that the first time he had appeared at the Sayre residence in Montgomery, he had fallen into the hallway dead drunk. Her sister Zelda, said the writer of this troubled letter, would have been saved a life of pain and notoriety if she never had seen young Scott again.

While personal feeling as intense as this deserves our compassion, it is futile to deny Fitzgerald's claim on our attention. The price of his easily won but hard-kept fame is the need of the scholar, the public, and the friend to relate Fitzgerald's personal history to the body of his work. Scott's most famous friend and contemporary, Ernest Hemingway, has called "ghouls and gravediggers" those of us who, either through firsthand reminiscences or carefully researched biography, have concerned ourselves with the life and writings of Scott Fitzgerald. If this be true, then all biographers and authors of telling memoirs are ghouls and gravediggers, from Tacitus and Plutarch to Carl Sandburg and Bruce Catton. If Flaubert or Byron or Poe had friends who loved them, or intimates who despised them, but in any case closely observed them, these associates had a right, even a responsibility, to share their experiences with posterity. And if Flaubert was a mama's boy, Byron a rake, and Poe an addict and a drunk, who is to say that these facts—especially as reported firsthand—do not belong in the hero's catalogue along with the demonstrable virtues?

Hemingway—whose friendship with Fitzgerald was complex and ambivalent when it was not downright mean—may have referred to us as "gravediggers" out of latent fear that we might discover Scott's skeleton in his own closet. As noted earlier, Fitzgerald supported Hemingway in the middle twenties when the former was already a public figure while the latter was still an indigent discovery of the little magazines. Although Hemingway thanked Fitzgerald privately for this act of fraternal generosity, he could never bring himself to public acknowledgment of Fitzgerald's literary encouragement that had come to Papa in its most tangible form—a flow of one-hundred-dollar checks! Hemingway paid off his old friend with the back of his hand. The sentient quality of *A Moveable Feast* is marred by his cruel and petty anecdotes about his erstwhile benefactor and friend.

For Ernest, apparently, it was not a question of whether or not to dig up Scott's bones but of who did the digging.

Hemingway's attitude toward Scott always had been an amalgam of admiration and contempt. One of the deep wounds had been his criticism of *Tender Is the Night* as a piece of work that was not really a novel because it drew so explicitly on the Fitzgeralds themselves and their experiences with the Gerald Murphys and their other mutual friends on the Cap d'Antibes. Fitzgerald could have said the same thing about *The Sun Also Rises*. Around the Café Dôme, after the publication of that explosive novel, habitués began to call each other by the names Hemingway had assigned their fictitious alter egos. Hemingway seemed to apply a double standard to himself and Fitzgerald: what he put down about his friends was serious work—what Scott wrote was personal confession. He was characteristically unable to empathize with Scott or to see his work in any true perspective.

Nietzschean nature boys like Ernest and Jack London have trouble with more subtle, urbanized personalities like Scott's. Our existential, hard-boiled American artists have no patience with the introspection and self-examination of a faltering but struggling Scott Fitzgerald. They come on with a kind of *Me-Tarzan!* bravado that abhors weakness and pushes their own weakness as far back into their gut as they can hide it. Their nexus is power, megalomania, and suicide. The gun, in life and in death, was as essential to the psyche of Ernest Hemingway as it is to any self-respecting and self-determined Black Panther. The Fitzgeralds on the other hand are committed to nonviolence, to the stoic if self-pitying endurance of their wounds, and to marginal survival. Ernest and Scott would have to be critical of each other's manner of escape from this mortal coil. The sense of domination that gave Hemingway's writing that marvelous tension was also a superior's contempt for human failings that made it impossible for Ernest not to become increasingly patronizing toward Scott as the latter insisted on immolating himself in "bad times" while the former equally insisted on insulating himself in "good times." You can learn to live with bad times but never with good times gone rotten. There was a tiny core of toughness hidden in Fitzgerald's weaknesses, just as there was a tiny core of weakness hidden in Hemingway's strengths. So it was understandable that Ernest would keep firing away at Scott's "weaknesses," just as it is understandable he should feel that Scott's bones belonged to him by right of antecedence. And also by the supreme right of Number One-ism. Believing himself the champion writer of the land, he assumed that any subject he might be interested in became his private preserve. Thus he would resent as an incursion on his rights any novel about prizefighting or about war or about fishing or bullfighting, or about a Fitzgerald prototype in the twenties. Even this might have been acceptable if Hemingway had been prepared to have the last word on Fitzgerald and if he had been big enough to make that last word generous and true. But on these two counts he failed, attempting instead to bully us into accepting his own first word—or judgment—as the final word for all. And so, if Papa will permit, we would wish not to disturb the grave but to lay another wreath upon it, by putting into words as accurately as mind allows, our remembering of Scott Fitzgerald.

Our meeting in the Goldwyn Studio early in 1939 still holds for me a dreamlike, legendary quality. Even while it was happening I felt as if the gods had swooped down and carried me off to serve as a minor player in one of their more extravagant myths. As a recent Dartmouth graduate and novice screenwriter I had been engaged by an older son of Dartmouth, Walter Wanger, to write a screenplay against the background of Winter Carnival. It was before the day when teen-age lovers held stage center, and Mr. Wanger felt that a mature love story (starring Ann Sheridan and Richard Carlson) should be woven prominently into the tapestry. There I had faltered and Mr. Wanger had decided that I needed an older hand with whom to collaborate. Who would this older hand be? "Scott Fitzgerald," said Mr. Wanger, pretty casually, it seemed to me even then.

I'm not sure if my quickening pulse was perceptible. But across the gulf of three decades I can still remember the shock of reaction to that name. Although Fitzgerald was not one of our Writers' Congress gods of the thirties, not Steinbeck nor Farrell, Malraux nor Hemingway, he had become an off-horse favorite of mine. I had savored *The Great Gatsby* for form and style in college, and I knew the best of the wonderfully evocative short stories, *May Day* and *The Rich Boy* and *Crazy Sunday*. And, drawn to its incomparable texture, I had read and reread *Tender Is the Night*. I was something of a literary schizo, a loyal *New Masses* subscriber and at the same time a literary freewheeler who could admire Faulkner even if he was "reactionary" or Fitzgerald if he was "decadent," as they were both dismissed by the Party littérateurs.

When Walter Wanger mentioned Fitzgerald now, I remembered having been introduced to him by Dorothy Parker, coming out of the Biltmore Theater in downtown Los Angeles three years earlier. It had been a surprise to learn he was living in Hollywood. My fleeting image was of a gray ghost with a wan smile, under a shapeless gray fedora. Then, in the excitement of young love, young politics, and a youthful enthusiasm for short-story and screen writing, my image of Fitzgerald had faded. That is why, when Mr. Wanger suggested that I might collaborate with him, I exclaimed (for this part of the myth is true), "My God, I thought Scott Fitzgerald was dead!" To which Mr. Wanger had replied, "Not unless your treatment bored him to death. He's in the next office reading it now."

Looking back, it is difficult to realize that the Scott Fitzgerald I saw that day was still a relatively young man in his early forties. To my callow eyes of 1939, he looked more like sixty. There is, of course, a patronizingly faulty time-machine in the minds of the young which transforms the most robust of middle-aged men into septuagenarians. But Scott Fitzgerald, with his pale and ghostly look, made his own contribution to this

illusion. There seemed to be no colors in him. The proud, somewhat too-handsome profile of his earlier dust-jackets was crum-
pled. To this day I am unable to say exactly what it was that left
me with this lasting impression. The fine forehead, the leading
man's nose, the matinee-idol set of the gentle, quick-to-smile
eyes, the good Scotch-Irish cheekbones, the delicate, almost
feminine mouth, the tasteful, Brooks Brothers attire—he had
lost none of these. But there seemed to be something physically
or psychologically broken in him that had pitched him forward
from scintillating youth to shaken old age.

Much of what happened to us in the cataclysmic weeks to
follow has either been roughly described or folded into other
experiences with various other writers in *The Disenchanted*.
So I shall try to telescope those weeks so as to leave room for
my memories of him in his post-Carnival final year-and-a-half.
My encounter with Sinclair Lewis four years earlier had found
Red at the height of his fame—if not of his powers—a rich, outwardly self-assured, world-famous figure. Scott's case was
altogether different. In fact, his was the opposite face on the flip-
coin of success-in-failure, failure-in-success. He had, in a way,
written his own obituary—at least as a public figure—in the pages
of *Esquire* magazine.* His books were out of print, his reputation was out of joint, his financial situation was out of kilter.
Lewis, though I was to find some telltale cracks in that richly
successful façade, was the very model of a modern major literary celebrity. Scott, alas, was a kind of dilapidated Model-A
roadster, once as shiny and jazzy as they came but now neglected and condemned by public apathy to the used-car lots.
Red Lewis, for instance, while acknowledging that I was a member of a new generation he ought to "look into," took it as his
due that I was conversant with his work and Carol Kennicott,
Martin Arrowsmith, and Sam Dodsworth were part of my vo-

* "The Crack-Up," "Handle with Care," and "Pasting It Together," a
series of heart-breaking revelations, painfully naked, heroic in their deter-
mination to put the pieces back together and salvage what was left of
squandered genius.

cabulary. But while Lewis was still riding the crest of the wave, Scott had been swept deep into the trough and he was flattered and stimulated and, it seemed to me, pathetically pleased to find any product of the Depression thirties who remembered, admired, and could talk *Gatsby* or *Tender*.

He struck me not as a totally defeated but more as a proud and embattled failure, fully, almost vaingloriously aware of his place in American letters and still deeply wounded by the public and critical rejection of *Tender Is the Night*. Throughout the twenties he had been the darling of both the littérateurs and the populace; then in the thirties, when just about everything was falling away from him, they had rudely deserted him. The shock might have destroyed a lesser talent. Scott was an odd mixture of insufficient stamina and marathon durability, as he was to demonstrate in the punishing months that lay ahead.

For days and days, when we were supposed to be working out a new story line for *Winter Carnival* (for which we kept trying to whip up some spurious enthusiasm), we talked: about his work, about Hollywood, about politics, about the cultural ebb and flow of succeeding generations, about moviemaking. Unlike my Manley Halliday* in *The Disenchanted,* Scott was quite the opposite of a film snob. In fact, he had plunged into a study of film-making that even included a card file of the plot lines of all the pictures he had seen. Although he thought of himself, naturally, as a novelist first and last, he was not in film work, like so many novelists and playwrights I had known, only for the fat Hollywood checks he needed to get back to his own line. He liked pictures and felt his talent was well suited to the medium. As early as 1925, after the publication of *The Great Gatsby,* he had given Max Perkins, his editor at Scribner's, a case of the fits by suggesting that he was considering giving up the novel for a film career. That must have been like Nijinsky telling Diaghilev he was thinking of turning in his ballet slippers for the metallic shoes of a tap

* A composite of *all* the walking-wounded novelists and playwrights I had been observing through my years of growing up in Hollywood.

dancer. For the next fifteen years Fitzgerald could never quite disengage himself from the dream of the great future awaiting him at the end of the Hollywood rainbow. Always something of a seer who could read the future in the shifting American values, he was able to anticipate the language of the visual that would become the mother tongue of the counter-culture adopted by the rock- and film-oriented kids of the sixties and seventies. Of course, he was drawn to the power and glamour of the "movie world," for which even at his advanced age he was able to maintain a boyish enthusiasm. But it was because he cared about the scripts he had worked on at M-G-M—unlike most of the cynical New York writers who holed up at the Garden of Allah—that he suffered when those scripts were wrenched away from him and rewritten by producers and writers he considered his inferiors. Like Mark Twain and Jack London, and so many other creative spirits who trapped themselves within the money-ridden society their minds rejected, he carried with him the American tragedy of being a serious artist who aspired to the largest possible audience, a writer who needed a constant stream of gold to pay off his debts and get back to his fiction. At the same time Scott was a movie fan who believed in film as an ideal art form for reaching out to millions who might never read a serious novel.

This ideal had been seriously shaken, he confessed, by his experience on *Three Comrades,* a screenplay he had been proud of until his producer Joe Mankiewicz had taken it away from him, rewritten the dialogue, and, in Scott's opinion, dulled its cutting edge.

Joe Mankiewicz had been brought to Hollywood by my father, on the recommendation of his brilliant older brother Herman, and both of them had impressed my old man as being among the more literate and inventive writers in "the industry." Scott said he knew Mank (as Herman was always called) very well and considered him a kind of spoiled priest who might have been a genius if he had not become so preoccupied with the private life of Hollywood—some of his best work seemed to go into malicious jokes at the expense of his producers and fellow writers during long, liquid lunches at Romanoff's. And he thought younger brother Joe was longer on discipline but shorter on talent. If the latter had supported him, Scott told me, instead of feeling he had to compete with him as a writer, *Three Comrades* would have been a film that lived up to and perhaps even surpassed the Remarque novel.*

That, I said, was the nature of this town. Since I had been brought up in the place, I had no illusions about it. I had learned from intelligent producers, like Irving Thalberg, David Selznick, and my own father, that even the wisest of them looked upon the screenwriter as low man on the totem pole.

We talked *pictures,* but we also talked *Hollywood.* I was happy to find a subject I knew more about than he did, and he listened as well as he talked. Both of us were intensely interested in the history or development of the despised nickelodeon Cinderella of 1909 now going to the ball in the golden coach of 1939. It was difficult for me to think of Hollywood as *Hollywood,* I told him, because I grew up on its streets, helped build underground clubhouses in its vacant fields and attended its public schools. It was simply *home town.* I used to ride my bike up Vine Street when it was still lined with pepper trees, and hike in the Hollywood hills when there was nothing up there but the Hollywoodland sign and the old Hollywood hermit who lived in a lean-to behind the sign. Scott found those early days fascinating. He wanted to know more about my father, B.P., one of the last of the big-studio bosses in the flam-

---

* In fairness to Joe Mankiewicz, it should be stated that *Three Comrades* won favorable notices from most of the critics and inclusion in "The Ten Best Pictures" of 1939. But in fairness to Scott, a line of *his* describing the comrades' jerry-built racing car ("The grandpa was a sewing machine, the grandma was an old radio and the papa was a machine gun") was softened by the substitution of "an alarm clock" for the gun. Scott's line used atmosphere as a dramatic threat. In the Germany of the twenties not only was there makeshift fun and games but also incipient violence. Old machine guns relegated to the scrap heaps lived on in other contraptions. Scott felt his employer had gone for the easy laugh at the expense of sharp truth, and that this was typical of their conflicting approaches to the film.

boyant days of Clara Bow and Marlene Dietrich, both of whom he had brought to Hollywood. And what did I think about Thalberg, Mayer, and the other tycoons?

Although Scott had been raked severely by the critics for his "escapist attitude," "his self-deceiving identification with the wastrel rich," I was surprised to find that he talked more like a confirmed leftist, anti-Stalinist but Marxist-oriented. Here again he was at the opposite end of the spectrum from Sinclair Lewis, who said a loud damn not only to both your houses but to all domiciles housing any one body of political thought. Nobody seemed able to influence Lewis, at least not for long, but Fitzgerald, as far back as his Princeton days, had looked to Edmund Wilson as his mentor or "conscience" in matters artistic, and in recent years he had followed that old friend into the alien fields of social consciousness. I had never met Mr. Wilson, but "Bunny," as Scott called him, was a constant companion and frame of reference in our conversations. There were two terrible gods in Scott's life: Bunny, the god of the mind, and Ernest (alias Papa), the god of the viscera. Rarely was there a conversation that did not defer to one or the other. Scott was temperamentally a worshiper of heroes, needing them as crutches to support his own frailty and self-doubt. From their first meeting Ernest had impressed Scott as a literary superman, physically and artistically formidable, while Scott was physically and artistically vulnerable. Scott's attitude toward Ernest was reverential. But on those occasions when *El Formidable* pushed *El Vulnerable* to the wall, the awe-struck victim would, almost apologetically, hit back at the bullyboy tactics of his hero. It was, as Scott revealed himself, a classic example of the love-hate relationship that inevitably eroded an intriguing friendship.

In his memorable *Esquire* story, *The Snows of Kilimanjaro*, Ernest had written off "poor Scott" as "wrecked," but Scott's instinct for survival was reflected in a keen, in fact heatedly partisan interest in contemporary history. Of course this was early 1939, the heyday of Hitler, and you might say any civilized man would be war- and Nazi-conscious. Still, some of our most distinguished Americans, from Lindbergh to Dreiser, were isolationists, whereas Scott was a confirmed and dedicated internationalist who followed the day-to-day progress and retrogression of the democratic cause and spoke feelingly and knowledgeably about the need for collective security if the Axis was to be denied.

With politics, Hollywood, American writing, Scott's own work and the plight of illustrious writers trapped in the film industry, at least a dozen of them our mutual friends—you may imagine how much work we accomplished on *Winter Carnival* in those congenial first few days. Red Lewis and I had talked the nights away, too. But for all his *dammit-to-hells* and *have-another drink, Budd,* I was always aware of Red's status. My first day with Scott was far more reserved, due to his Southern-style courtliness and my awe-struck inhibitions. But after the first few days of our imprisonment Scott warmed up and I relaxed and soon felt closer to him than I ever had to Lewis. Of course I was a few years older now, had published a dozen short stories in national magazines, and was a promising rookie professional. But Scott's character was the deciding factor. Scott met you (me) on equal terms. No matter how provoked, Scott would never have precipitated a scene at the Dartmouth Junto meeting like the blow-up with Lewis. After three or four days I began to think of him as a friend. Lewis, on the other hand, had been friendly, a famous writer who was both lonely and being nice to an earnest young man.

While Scott and I were beginning to know each other, the storm clouds gathered. Mr. Wanger wanted us to attend the Dartmouth Winter Carnival along with a camera crew, to guide that crew on how to shoot background and color material according to our outline in the absence of a shooting script. Also, it would be an opportunity for Scott to refresh his memory on the facts of life in the Ivy League. In vain did Scott protest that his memory was quite adequate to the subject. And that he did not feel strong enough to make the trip. Why not send me as his deputy? I could take notes for him and advise the crew. The two of us, he said, had established excellent rapport. He would keep working on the revision during the week Mr. Wanger and I were away and—but Wanger interrupted him. Our producer was adamant. Scott's presence in Hanover was essential to the success of this project. Scott and I glanced at each other and, as we say now, got the message. Walter Wanger was a Dartmouth dropout with intellectual pretensions and box-office ambitions. He smoked a pipe, looked down on illiterate Hollywood producers, and liked to show off his books. Even a déclassé Scott Fitzgerald would be a calling card on the Dartmouth College academicians. The nervous eyes of W.W. were insistent. I felt a flicker of defeat in Scott's reluctant acquiescence.

And so we were on our way. My father, ever a sport and excited at the thought of my collaborating with F. Scott Fitzgerald, came to the airport to see me off with two magnums of vintage champagne. As soon as we were airborne I urged Scott to join me in a toast. At first he demurred. But after a little more persuading we touched paper cups and drank to our new-found friendship and—God help us!—*Winter Carnival*.

Other toasts followed, both serious and frivolous, as we talked our way into that long night's journey. It was a fifteen-hour flight in those days with stops for refueling. Our mood was half holiday, half panic. Scott reminisced about Bunny Wilson, the pervasive Ernest, Ring Lardner, Carl van Vechten, Gertrude Stein . . . He defended the esthetic values of his generation with such conviction that I have promoted his argument ever since: along with its flappers and bootleg gin and a sense of wasteful carnival, the mid-twenties was actually a period of unprecedented artistic vitality. In 1925 alone, when *The Great Gatsby* confirmed Scott as the Prodigy of American letters, other books published that year included Dreiser's *An American Tragedy,* Dos Passos' *Manhattan Transfer,* Lewis's *Arrowsmith,* Hemingway's astonishing collection of short stories, *In Our Time* (with *The Sun Also Rises* close behind). Faulkner was beginning, Frost was coming into his maturity, O'Neill had a new play ready every season, Dorothy Parker was at the top of her Emily Dickinsonian form, Ring Lardner's latest book of short stories was coming off the presses, and there were volumes of poetry by Ezra Pound, Archibald MacLeish, Edwin Arlington Robinson, Amy Lowell . . . the list went on. Not to mention the movies, Chaplin and all the wonderful silent comedians. Nineteen twenty-five had been a vintage year, no doubt about it. And every one of the years rounding out the twenties had produced a clutch of masterpieces. Once they broke through the Victorian curtain into the free new air of the postwar generation, there had been a kind of Vesuvian release of creative energy. All those people who went around crying "Lost!" had actually found themselves in the vigor and originality of their work.

There was something depressing and wrong about Scott's speaking up for the twenties as if it were his only muse. For as I tried to say that night as we bounced our way through the Middle Western darkness, though the thirties had been for him a dead season that had thoughtlessly neglected and abandoned him, it was still the decade that saw publication of *Tender Is the Night,* a book that John O'Hara, Dorothy Parker, and a lot of us believed would eventually come into its own. And the thirties had given us the best of Dos Passos, the *U.S.A.* trilogy. And there was *To Have and Have Not* and the anxiously awaited novel on the Spanish Civil War to prove that Ernest was still very much with us. And those overblown but inimitable novels of Thomas Wolfe. We had young writers like O'Hara, Pep West, and Jerome Weidman, whom Scott admired. And Faulkner, by American standards, was a late bloomer. And of course Steinbeck, Farrell, Odets . . .

There I began to lose my disillusioned traveler. He seemed to resist these names as inventions of the left-wing movement intent on literary heroes. Well, maybe we had no single golden year to equal 1925, I argued through the wine, but of creative ferment we still had aplenty. And despite what he may have felt, or failed to feel, for Farrell and Steinbeck, and despite his insistence in the *Esquire* series that he was now a depleted recluse or has-been, he seemed to me far more clued in than Red Lewis had been to the issues of our time. One side of Fitzgerald, it's true, did seem to live constantly in the past. But when he came back to the present he seemed to me surprisingly contemporary. I use that adverb because whenever he returned to the present, after I had too hastily consigned him to a Huck Finn funeral, his curiosity about 1939 and his sensitivity to its currents continued to surprise me.

When we tired of comparing generations—a game for which we both seemed to have a special affinity—we took turns analyzing our "bookish" taskmaster, Walter Wanger. "Ivy on one side, California palm on the other," Scott said. We dissected the moguls of M-G-M, Thalberg, Mayer, and the gravel-voiced ex-bouncer Eddie Mannix, for whom Scott had worked on a series of humiliating fiascos. We devoted half an hour to David O. Selznick. It is a forgotten fact that Scott had been one of the writers on *Gone with the Wind* along with an incredible list that included Dorothy Parker, John Van Druten, Oliver H. P. Garrett, and a gaggle of other notables. I told Scott a Selznickism. Since my father had developed him as his assistant at Paramount, David thought it fitting that he should put me on the Selznick International payroll as soon as I got out of college: fifty dollars a week as a reader and "junior writer." Six months passed. Time for the option to skyrocket my weekly salary to a lofty seventy-five dollars. By this time I had written two full screenplays and half a dozen "originals" that had been dropped down a deep well of Selznickian silence. I sent David a note asking him as a personal favor *not* to pick up my option. At last, after long hours of "standing by," I was ushered into his spacious Colonial office. David was at the height of his fame and power then, a sort of latter-day Thalberg. My note had bruised his feelings and he grumbled that he was pretty disappointed in me. I grumbled back, with the license of having known him since boyhood, that I was pretty disappointed in him, too: all those months of writing scripts for the shelf without so much as a word from him! "I realize we've carried you on the roster as a writer," Selznick acknowledged, "but frankly,

I think you've shown damn little initiative. Why, when I was your age and working for your father, I flooded B.P. with memos, memos on casting, on story purchases, on cutting costs, on judicious cuts after previews—all day long I kept feeding a stream of memos over his desk. I must've written over a thousand of them. But you—I don't think you've sent me two memos since you've been here."

"But, David," I said, "that's where we're different. You were practicing to become a producer. I want to be a writer."

"Yes, I know," David Selznick said, his voice dulled with disappointment. "You told me you wanted to be a writer. But I felt if I kept you with me long enough, sooner or later your producer's blood would begin to assert itself."

"*Producer's blood* became a favorite family joke," I told Scott on the plane going East. "Whenever we suffered a slight scratch, drawing a drop or two of blood, my brother, sister, and I would always cry out, 'Producer's blood!'"

Scott laughed at the story and we swapped anecdotes lined with malice about producers, a favorite form of release therapy for embattled and embarrassed screenwriters. The second magnum of champagne was going the way of the first. We both felt giddy and talkative. The conversational gamut ran from Scott's desperation plan for revising and reviving *Tender Is the Night*—to put it in chronological sequence rather than beginning in the middle and then sweeping back to incorporate past events as in the original novel*—to his opinion of Earl Browder, our American Communist leader, whom Scott

---

* A dozen years later Scribner's finally acceded to Scott's wishes that the novel be republished in his revised version. Typically, it appeared a decade too late for Scott to see his book back in circulation as he had hoped and begged. My review for *The New York Times* only elaborated on what I had told Scott on the flight that night—*Tender* was a fascinating novel, one of the most haunting ever written by an American, and I preferred it the way it was, before the "improvements." Frantic to find the reason for its failure, Scott had been clutching at straws in hope of blowing new life into it. His confidence had been badly shaken but the basic flaw lay with the public and the critics. The times were out of joint with Scott, not vice versa. Forces greater than his, but not truer, had decided that this was not to be his season of success.

diagnosed as a know-nothing Kansan who provided the perfect "popular front" for Soviet policies; from his early championship of Ernest Hemingway, whom he still believed in as the master truth teller, to his contempt for what he considered the ruined talents of Dorothy Parker, John Howard Lawson, Donald Ogden Stewart, and others who used Hollywood and Communism as outlets for their own artistic failures. I was, of course, closer to the Communists than Scott (indeed at that time still a secret member), and I felt rather fond and comradely toward Don and Dotty, although I already had had a foretaste of my troubles with Lawson, who had started off as a promising forerunner to Odets with such plays as *Processional* and *Success Story,* then had become a hard-nosed functionary who had surrendered all the originality he ever had to Party discipline and did his zealous best to impose the strictures of Stalinist art on the fellow writers he dominated.* Edmund Wilson's attitude toward these people—and Scott's aspirations beyond the college house-party movie that was dragging him East . . . oh, there was enough to talk about to keep us busy through the night. Occasionally we even managed to get around to *Winter Carnival.* When we got to the hotel, we assured each other, when we had cleaned up and had a solid meal, we promised ourselves, we would bear down on this assignment and the story line would come into focus.

In the Hotel Warwick we sent down for steak sandwiches and a bottle of whiskey, wrestled with our story for a jumble of hours, and then, since this was my first trip to New York in three years, or since my undergraduate days, I was eager to look up a few old friends. I asked Scott if he minded. Not at all, he would take a long bath and then make some notes on our story alone. He was not accustomed to writing in tandem, and perhaps he would make more progress if he had an hour or two to think it out on his own. Then he could use me for a sounding board when I returned. Happily passing the buck to

* Ironically, his *Theory and Technique of Playwriting* is one of the few helpful "how-to" books in the field of dramaturgy.

my senior partner, I found my friends and tarried for an extra, convivial hour. It was the last taste of well-being I would have on this trip. When I got back to our suite, pleasantly high, there was no sign of Scott. Then I found a scrawled handwritten note on my bed. "Pal you shouldn't have left me pal because I got lonely pal and went down to the bar pal and started drinking pal and now you may never find me pal . . ."

In a panic I ran down to the hotel bar. Yes, the man I was looking for had been there for about an hour. He had gone out just a short time ago.

I looked into one bar after another until I found Scott farther down the street. A frightening change had taken hold of him. We got back to the room. Black coffees. Cold showers. I apologized. Scott apologized. We promised each other to work, *work*. In an exhausted, distraught state, we tried. All night and into the early morning we tried. Later that morning we were to report to Mr. Wanger in his suite in the Waldorf Towers to tell him our story. We had been two days without sleep, and even my young, healthy constitution was beginning to run down. The atmosphere was tense. Walter Wanger looked groomed and rested. By way of easy openers he asked us if we had met anyone we knew on the plane. There was a hole in the conversation and I decided to fill it. "Let's see, oh yes, Sheilah Graham was on the plane," I said. Quite casually—it had seemed to me—we had encountered the handsome, peaches-and-cream-complexioned British Hollywood gossip writer sitting a number of rows behind us. She and Scott had seemed politely surprised and pleased to discover each other going East on the same plane. Scott had introduced her to me and then we had gone back to our seats. That's all it was, so far as I knew. But now, when I mentioned the columnist's name, Walter Wanger fixed Scott with a very strange look. "Scott, you son of a bitch," he said with a taut, disapproving smile.

On our way out, after a rather disastrous story conference, I turned to my besieged collaborator and said, "Holy God,

Scott, I'm terribly sorry. I never would have mentioned her if I had—"

"All my fault," Scott said. "I should have told you. Maybe it's just as well it's out in the open with Walter, anyway. I don't know why I feel I have to hide things from him like a schoolboy . . ."

It was in the nature of this basically unnatural relationship, we agreed. When had writers—not willing hacks but *real writers*—hired out as indentured literary servants? For a writer to work not *with* someone, which is difficult but possible as we see in the theater, but *for* someone is to enter the slave quarters or the kindergarten. You find yourself falling into all the familiar ploys of inferior status. First you fib to your producer and then you begin to lie. You play hookey. You rebel in all sorts of little ways that satisfy your immature sense of defiance. You stick your tongue out at Daddy behind his back. You resent being on an allowance and yet you are terrified to be without it. When Walter Wanger asked us how we were coming along with his story we did not tell him the truth—for fear of being fired. Disinherited. No, the children, even the famous if fallen writer of *The Great Gatsby* and *Tender Is the Night*, like a string of distinguished novelists and playwrights I had been watching and pitying all my life, had to stall and make excuses and do their best to put one over on Papa. You lie and then you laugh nervously at your nursery school or chain-gang disingenuousness and then you work desperately and guiltily to change the lie into at least a half truth that will get you through another day.

Back at the Warwick, sucking on our bottle like two overgrown kids, we exchanged confidences about our salaries. Scott was being paid fifteen hundred dollars a week, the most he had ever made. I was making two hundred and fifty dollars a week, a small fortune on which I was secretly hoping to repair to the Vermont woods and try to write a novel. Neither of us saw *Winter Carnival* as anything but a meal ticket to some fuller life. In a sense we were both taking money under false pretenses. We had never had any illusions about this little valentine for Walter Wanger. It was simply a job, a good job, for me a chance to revisit Dartmouth, and now as a bonus, a chance to work with F. Scott Fitzgerald. My own spirit was much tougher and meaner than this story called for. And Scott's was finer and far more subtle. What invariably happens when writers try to write down to their material is that they don't do it as convincingly as the writers who really believe in that material. The Hollywood hills were crawling with competent "B writers" who could have banged out a sentimental entertainment for Ann Sheridan without pain or hesitation. But Scott really tried, in a manic way, urged on by alcohol, and I tried to help him try.

There had been another last-minute request for a reprieve. Scott had phoned Walter to ask if he might not spend the weekend at the hotel working on our desperately needed story line while I went north on the Carnival Special to reconnoiter for local color on the Dartmouth front and relay my intelligence to our command post at the Warwick. It was the sensible move, for Scott had begun the journey in weakened condition and was now clearly in no state for a trip to the Hanover snows. But our Master's Voice insisted that we be on the Special, and so we limped aboard, the gray colors of our suits and our dispositions contrasted to the bright colors and flirtatious laughter of the Carnival dates ready for the weekend of their young lives.

The girls were a dazzling array, and before we had passed through the first parlor car our dapper tycoon had spotted at least three future Toby Wings he wanted to test for our picture. This had once been Scott's scene, his domain, but now he lagged slowly behind, insisting he had lived this all before, that he was not going to walk through the entire train ogling the pretty children like a lecherous old man and that, Wanger or no Wanger, he was returning to our compartment. I followed him back to the end of the aisle, where he fished from his pocket a pint bottle of gin. How Scott managed to procure that gin bottle, while we had been practically handcuffed together since the night before, I never learned. Leaving Scott to his contemplation of the winter landscape, I hurried to catch up with Walter.

Our producer interrupted his enthusiastic talent hunt to ask me a direct question. "Budd, I want you to tell me the truth. Has Scott been drinking?"

Since our take-off from Burbank we had been awash in fervid discussion and a constant flow of refreshments. "Well, we've had a few drinks—to keep working," I said, hearing the echo of my own insufficient lie.

Walter swore softly. "His agent gave me his word of honor he was on the wagon for good. Go back and keep an eye on him. For God's sake don't let him drink any more."

Exactly how I was to accomplish this feat, our benefactor did not explain. I went back to find Scott surrounded by a group of recent Dartmouth graduates, whose youth and vigor made my sorry author look like a washed-out eighty-three rather than a man who should have been in the prime of life at forty-three. There was trouble brewing. One of the young visitors was a handsome blond football star whose chemistry had begun to clash with Scott's. Like so many of our generation, the football player identified Fitzgerald with the follies of the twenties. He said that he had read *Gatsby* in college and considered it an overrated novel. Scott had never wanted to be on this train in the first place and now one of his last props was being knocked from under him. Of course it wasn't fair, and at the same time, as I was to learn along the way, with his genius not only for self-creating but for self-destroying, he had asked for it. He had introduced himself by asking if they realized that he was F. Scott Fitzgerald—an immodesty, I learned later, he indulged only when he was potted. And then, in a pathetic effort to stand off the jibes of the football player, he had questioned this apprentice corporation lawyer as to how much he earned a week and then trumped him by boasting that he made ten times that much. And the football player had retaliated—"The great Scott Fitzgerald—a Hollywood hack!"

At this point, outweighed by seventy-five pounds and looking about fit enough to last perhaps five seconds of the first round, Scott challenged his brawny tormentor to a fist fight. Scott came from the old school, with a dash of Southern chivalry, and believed in defending himself against ungentlemanly slurs. In a noisy pushing match we finally managed to clear the compartment.

We would be arriving at Dartmouth early in the morning. The camera crew would be descending on us, asking what action to shoot as background for particular scenes. And Walter Wanger, on the prowl, with his shifty cat eyes, would be waiting for his story. Already battered and bedraggled, objects of derision from my frisky contemporaries (I think I resented them their youth as much as Scott did that long-ago winter night), we promised each other not to discuss Hemingway or Steinbeck, not to analyze Walter Wanger, not to mention Edmund Wilson and his anti-Communist communism, not to exchange our impressions of the Hollywood assembly-line system, not to think about any of a hundred things that seemed to fascinate us both—not to say anything for the next two hours that did not relate directly to the root cause of this mad journey, *Winter Carnival*. And so we hurtled through the night, jettisoning one poor plot after another as our brains reeled on.

At some point in the small hours, with the delusion of the desperate, we thought we were making progress. And progress calls for black coffee. But the diner was long closed. The train groaned to a stop. Where? Springfield? Bernardston? Brattleboro? We never knew. Through the compartment window our bleary eyes recognized an all-night diner beyond the station platform. Hot coffee to sober us and keep us awake with bright ideas! We hurried across the street and into the diner. With a wary eye on our Carnival Special we ordered coffee in a hurry, drank another cup, and then, wild as it sounds, when Scott insisted on paying the check, all of eighty cents for coffee and donuts to blot up the booze, he discovered that he had lost his paycheck. Why was he carrying a check for fifteen hundred dollars? He had planned to deposit it when we got to New York, but of course we had never had time. Perhaps he liked the power of it in his pocket. Anyway, we couldn't find it. We both flailed around in frantic search. Scott was positive he had had it with him when he left the train. The train blew a warning whistle. I turned, caught sight of the damned check between the bar stool and the counter, and dove for it. Psychologists, make of this what you will. We made a run for the train but as in a nightmare when you know you are running running toward futility, we were on the platform when the train began to move. We ran alongside it, calling, begging, but it did not hear us and moved on into the night. It was a night of snow, of swirling blizzard, and like the rest of this improbable but surrealistically predictable trip, full of constant surprise. We found an old man to drive us in an old car cold as an icebox and we kept warm by huddling together and drinking from a bottle (whiskey this time) and singing. We sang a lot on that trip. We laughed a lot because we were so miserable. We raced the train. Icy roads. We didn't expect to die. It was more like Captain Stormfield's visit to heaven. We were dead and enjoying the trip. Such suffering as we endured that frozen morning can only be endured with gritted laughter. We drew ahead of the train and reached the next station platform, where the train was not even scheduled to stop. But somehow we waved it down. I doubt if that would happen now. Hell, there isn't even a *train* to Dartmouth any more. Waved it down and reboarded, about three o'clock in the morning. Two shivering ghosts who had lifted off from the lights of Hollywood two days or light-years before. Surrealism rode that train to Hanover. At five o'clock Scott had a brainstorm. He saw "the whole picture" in a poetic vision. All he had was an opening. *Five* of the hundred minutes we were in cold pursuit of. He felt this was Eureka. I thought it was an eloquent piece of prose poetry. He wanted to push the buzzer of Walter's drawing room and tell him "the story." I wanted us to coast into Dartmouth, try to clean up and sober up while Walter got involved in the festivities of arrival. Scott was hurt. He made another chivalric thing out of it. If I did not stand shoulder to shoulder with him, he would go on alone. What to do? My heart was dragging but we went together. After a long wait Walter opened the door. Scott told him we had solved his story. Walter did not look so dapper with his eyes full of sleep and his mouth wanting teeth. There was a moment's hesitation. Perhaps this is the way genius strikes—at five o'clock in the morning on a train racing through the icy dark of New England.

Now he was the distinguished Dartmouth producer with the author of *The Great Gatsby*. "Fine, Scott, I'd like to hear it." A pause. Scott turned to me. "Budd, why don't you tell it." I suggested we all go back to sleep (*back* was the height of hyperbole) and meet at the Hanover Inn in the late morning. I kept hoping and half believing we would come up with something that would *work* if only we had a little more time. But now that Walter was awake he insisted. I deferred to Scott and he went into the same lovely nonsense he had tried on me. Walter wasn't sure. Truth was, for all his pretense Walter had no story mind at all. So it was agreed that we review the situation at his suite at the Inn as soon as we were bathed and unpacked.

We staggered back to our compartment, closed our eyes for what seemed like five minutes, arrived to the sound of feminine squeals and young laughter, and, ready or not, were catapulted into Carnival.

Only in some improbable fantasy would it have seemed possible for the film company to have forgotten to make reservations for us at the Inn, so that Walter Wanger could enjoy a spacious suite overlooking the campus while we were relegated to a makeshift maid's room in the attic devoid of furniture except for a metal double-decker bed and a single hard chair. "A perfect symbol of the writer's status in Hollywood," Scott described those neglected quarters, where for two days we fumed, labored, drank, suffered icy research, nerve-wracking deadlines, humiliating public receptions, and our climactic melodramatic defeat.

In some masochistic way not uncommon to indentured Hollywood writers, we enjoyed Scott's nifty summary of our condition. One of the things that impressed me most in the course of that arctic weekend hell was the quality of Scott's creative intelligence and the courage of his humor. He was constantly noticing little things that amazed me—details of the academic life as exact as the lexicon of O'Hara. The lids may have drooped, and the hand trembled, but the eye of the novelist never wavered.

There was to be a faculty reception for us in the social room of the Inn and we were discussing whether or not to attend when we had a visitor, one of my favorite sociology professors, Francis ("Red") Merrill. In my undergraduate days, Red, a social scientist drawn to the arts, designed a special course for me on the Sociology of the American Novel. A Dartmouth athlete in the twenties, Red had been fascinated by Scott's evocation of the era. And although he was also a great fan of Hemingway's, he shared my feeling that Hemingway had developed a tantalizing use of the American language for the distillation of experience but that when we appraised them as novelists we found Scott the more searching and satisfying.

To celebrate this double occasion, my homecoming and his meeting with Scott, Red unwittingly brought us the gift we needed least, a bottle of whiskey. However, we welcomed it as a gift from Dionysus and drank it together, discussing the novel of the twenties while we cranked or drank up our courage to go down and face the official reception.

There seems to be a cruel joy lurking in insular and self-righteous people who resent fame and accomplishments beyond their own boundaries of Academe. The appearance on campus of a poet or novelist in a state of disarray gives them reassurance, justifies their retreat from the traps and cannon fire of the outside world. But that afternoon in the genteel confines of the Hanover Inn when the faculty and student onlookers were laughing at Scott, his accuracy toward them was muffled but deadly. In a slurred whisper behind his hand, he even discerned a Princeton man in the Dartmouth English Department—some special nattiness and sense of superiority to the barbaric brethren of New Hampshire had betrayed him to Scott at the very moment when this dapper prince was observing to me, "I was at Princeton about ten years after him. What a legend he was then! He's really all finished, isn't he?"

Crawling back to our attic haunt to reflect on our mutual deterioration, I remember periods of semihysterical laughter. The head of what Hollywood calls "the second unit," in charge of the camera crew Mr. Wanger had dispatched to cover the Winter Carnival, was an exuberant film technician by the name of Otto Lovering. As we had descended or fallen from the Carnival Special we had recognized "Lovey," but barely, disguised as a member of Admiral Peary's Polar expedition. Only his bright red nose had been visible in the great fur helmet crowning an Antarctic outfit that had transformed him into the Abominable Snowman. Lovey was Hollywood gung-ho—"Just tell me what you want—if you want us to go off the ski jump for a shot my boys'll get it—the best fuckin' crew in Hollywood —and they'll follow me anywhere. We don't care how fuckin' cold it is, we're ready to give it the old try-eroo!" A Marine Corps sergeant in World War I, Lovey had managed to carry this profane *esprit de corps* into his Hollywood assignments. In Wanger's presence Lovey was a respectful and virtually groveling lackey. But behind his producer's back, he was transformed into an anti-establishment tiger. After the reception, bursting into our attic vault in what we now called "his Eskimo suit," he said, "Look—to hell with Walter! He's so busy brownnosing those campus big shots he don't know shit from Shinola. So why don't the three of us just work close together and we'll get the fuckin' job done!"

Since we were still without a screenplay, we sent him on a wild-goose chase—photographing all the ice sculptures for an interfraternity contest we claimed to have outlined for the picture. Off into the snow he charged, lovable, dedicated, two-faced Lovey, in a burst of Hollywood-*cum*-Marine four-letter words that left us hanging onto each other in desperate laughter until we cried. Scott had never known a Lovey before, and I had been surrounded by them from the days of my Hollywood childhood. Lovey was to become "Robinson" in the mental notes Scott was making for *The Last Tycoon*. Oddly, we were both making notes on the idiosyncrasies of film production that would go into our respective Hollywood novels after we had done with *Winter Carnival*.

As I write this now I glance at a note from Scott that catches in a dozen words the mood and terror of that nightmare weekend. I had gone out with Lovey to point out some pictorial marvels for our nonexistent story. Meanwhile Walter had been pressing Scott to accompany him to some winter sports activities. At the desk, on a scrap of stationery bearing the printed legend, ". . . enjoy the Gay and Active Winter Season of The Hanover Inn," I found this message, "Budd: Am upstairs doing a sort of creative brood—Scott," with five terrible words appended: "Changed—gone out with Walter."

Selfishly, back in Hollywood I had wanted Scott Fitzgerald to come to Dartmouth with me. But I had not known the extent and hardly the existence of Scott's illness. Now I hurried out toward the ski jump, asking people along the way if they had seen Walter Wanger, Scott Fitzgerald—the Hollywood contingent. And finally I found him, trudging through the deep snow over the golf course in his baggy suit, his wrinkled overcoat and his battered fedora that refused to make the slightest sartorial concession to *Winter Carnival*. What a grim, gray joke he was to the young, hearty, rosy-cheeked Carnival couples in their multicolored ski clothes and their festive mating calls. I found them teasing Scott with the cruelty of children who torment the village idiot. Why Walter Wanger thought that Scott Fitzgerald needed to watch a host of young athletes flying through a valley of icy snow on long wooden staves in order to write a romantic comedy drama for Ann Sheridan remains one of those unsolved Hollywood mysteries. Somewhere in my files a faded snapshot of Scott on that peculiar occasion testifies to his physical inadequacy for that ordeal. Like children who beg to be excused from Phys Ed on the grounds that they have the sniffles, we asked Walter for permission to return to the Inn and continue what Scott had described rather optimistically as a "creative brood." Across the snow and back to the Inn we trudged, trying to ignore the catcalls of our tormentors. Scott felt a need to call Sheilah, to tell her the bad news that he had fallen off the wagon after eight heroic months—as if she didn't know. Then we retired to our attic where we made a desperation decision that Scott would concentrate on the old love story— the English professor and his lost lady—while I worked on young love, the ski captain and the college editor competing for the Carnival Queen. Somehow we would stitch our crazy quilt together. The fact that young love had been Scott's stock in trade for the *Saturday Evening Post* but that now I was to be his surrogate in these matters was an irony lost on neither of us that wintry evening. I was still close enough to them to care about college editors and the whim-whams of their dates. And Scott had been an excellent choice to write the story of old loves renewed—at the bottom of our creative trough there was always the feeling that we were after all the perfect team to bring this off—if only we could hold ourselves together.

To this end we decided on a nap. After an hour, with energy restored, we would pick up our lances in pursuit of the dragon of plot that had made itself invisible. Again I swung myself up onto the upper bunk while Scott sank down into the lower. A few minutes later I was called back from merciful unconsciousness by the sound of creaking springs. I looked down to see Scott rising from his pass-out funk on the metal cot and groping slowly toward the door.

"Scott? Where the hell are you going?"

"I'm going to Zelda. She needs me. I'm going to Zelda."

This was the first time he had mentioned his wife, who had helped to create the legend of the twenties, and whose mysterious breakdown in the thirties had dropped a dark, almost impenetrable curtain between them. I remember dragging him back from the door and throwing him down on the cot, hard. I remember his feeling frail and defenseless in my hands. I remember thinking he had passed out again and beginning to take off his shoes, and his reviving enough to say, "Oh, you must be enjoying yourself, feeling so strong, so young, so damn sure of yourself . . ." And I remember losing my patience and temper with him at last and running down the stairs and out through the lobby to Wheelock Street and over to the friendly Alpha Delta Phi fraternity bar, where I tried to drown our common sorrows and where, after fifteen minutes of troubled escapism, I felt a soft hand on my shoulder. Eerily, inescapably, the old ghost of many carnivals had tracked down his apprentice ghost.

He said something like, "Pal, you aren't going to desert your old pal now, are you, pal?" as if he were Scott playing Gatsby playing Scott, and I confess I felt guilty, as if I had tried to ditch a blind date who had turned out to be a "dog." Scott was right, we were in this together, the jibes and jabs of the revelers were aimed at both of us, and so we went out into the frozen Carnival night arm-in-arm, improvising scandalous songs about Walter Wanger and Lovey and "—where oh where is the funny funny faculty . . . ?"

We swung along Wheelock Street singing and laughing at the cleverness of our scatology like any other pair of Carnival celebrants. Magically, the Princeton professor materialized and Scott was able to pierce his armor of respectability and to tell him with a Merlinlike insight what he was really thinking. Cheered on by this triumph, Scott was now the handsome, hopeful sophomore on his way to the prom. In her book *Beloved Infidel* and in her talks with me afterward, Sheilah Graham has described Scott's drunkenness as a state of meanness and nastiness in which he even could become violent. I pretend to no expertise on this subject nor was it the intensely personal problem with which Sheilah had to cope. I write only what I saw and heard: for a man under the kind of creative, physical, and financial pressure Scott was suffering, he was incredibly good-natured, playful, and accepting. Maybe they were manic, but there were a lot of euphoric minutes braided through those dark hours. My on-again-off-again friend John O'Hara has described Scott as a difficult man to get along with but I never found that to be so. Then, and later, under circumstances that would drive most men to defensive malice, I saw Scott as a sick angel or a drunken angel or even a contrary and unpredictable angel, but I never saw him as vindictive as he might have been, considering that while he had admitted to being a poor caretaker of his talent, society had yet to admit that it had failed to respond to his many justified cries for help, or simply for professional support. All of this, of course, was to come later when the scholars and the critics (with a few honorable exceptions) were to rejoice in the rare butterfly they could add to their collection of glorified specimens.

But we are thinking now not of the dead hero but of the living target of critical faculty and undergraduate abuse, caroling along Wheelock Street singing silly songs of defiance. "Let's have a drink at the Psi U house!" Scott cried out like a stray from his own *Flappers and Philosophers*. We were arm in arm as we came abreast the Hanover Inn, where, to head off another binge, I tried to play a dirty trick on Scott. "Psi U house!" I said as I turned him in toward the steps to the lobby. He pulled away, rightly infuriated—"Get away from me!—You can't fool me!—I'll go there alone!"—and staggered on to the corner of Main Street. I pursued him and grabbed his arm—"Scott, we've got to go back to the room! In the morning we're supposed to tell our story to Walter and the whole goddamn Dartmouth brass! For Christ's sake, Scott!" He tried to pull away and I held on and the two of us spun around and went down into the snow. A two-horse sleigh went jingling by, leaving us in the wake of young laughter that Scott had described better than anybody else in the world. As we sat in the snow, we began to laugh at our predicament, helped each other to our feet, and decided to sober up with hamburgers and coffee at the Inn coffee shop and then on to our attic and back to work. Both of us felt apologetic, Scott for having wandered so far from the purpose of this outing, I for finally losing my patience with him and beginning to treat him like a typical drunk. We both solemnly promised to reform and on this note of sober intoxication, squeezed into an unoccupied nook in a coffee shop that was now a merry extension of all the fraternity house parties.

A middle-aged lady in a bright ski suit matched by a ruddy complexion and glowing smile called across to us and hurried over. Had we been looking for her? She had left a note at the Inn. Looking for her? For a moment we did not even remember her. Miss Holmquist! Packing for the Carnival Special, back at the Warwick, we suddenly had felt we needed a secretary to take down in shorthand and have neatly typed for Mr. Wanger the brilliant shavings of our mind that we would sweep into *Winter Carnival*. We had called down to the public stenographer at the desk, who said that since this was a weekend she could arrange to go herself.

"You know, all my life I've wanted to spend a weekend like this. I feel like a little girl in a fairy tale. If you need me, of course I'll be ready to take dictation. But if you're not going to work tonight, I met a very nice older man who has offered to take me to the Winter Sports Show." We told her we did not think we would need her services any more that evening but that she might be ready for an early start in the morning. "I don't know how I'll ever be able to thank you for all this!" she cried and melted back into the gaiety of the Carnival.

Scott's mood had turned upward. He suddenly decided he was ready to ad lib the *Winter Carnival* script. Now *Winter Carnival* became a surrealist film in which the slick surface of the ski jump dissolves to the slick surface of the faculty mind and then the smooth thigh of the Carnival Queen where the practical hand of our producer moves like a skier . . . It was a clever way of working off resentments and anxieties and I remember how we both laughed at Scott's facility in spinning out this Cocteau version of the Carnival kaleidoscope. But we both knew it was a game—we were equally drunk and sober at the same time—and so when the waitress brought us our check we decided on one more breath of winter air to clear our heads before returning to our lair. And if that happens to be a jingle, it truly reflects the second wind of hope that seemed to be restoring us. Around the corner to the entrance of the Inn we loped, and there on the steps, coming out to begin his evening, was our nemesis Walter Wanger, sober and elegant, standing several steps above us and wearing a top hat. The great cameraman Gregg Toland could not have lined it up more perfectly. We were not really doing anything explicitly wrong at that moment but we felt wrong and guilty and it showed in our dilapidation and on our woeful countenances.

"I don't know what time the next train goes to New York," spoke the voice of doom, "but you two are going to be on it." Someone volunteered the information that The Montrealer was coming through in half an hour. That would not even give us time to pack our bags, I protested. Walter said Lovey could bring them with him when he went down on Monday. Thus were we unceremoniously deposited on The Montrealer without our luggage, run out of town on a rail you might say. In adjoining roomettes and oblivions we hurtled back to New York. A tap on my shoulder from the Negro porter brought me back to semiconsciousness and the information that we were already in Pennsylvania Station—and also that my traveling companion could not be roused. I jumped up, having slept in those already much-slept-in clothes, and hurried in to Scott. His face was ashen and he did not stir. He had fallen into that frightening void between sleep and something more final. Together the porter and I lifted him from the bunk and half-carried him to the end of the train. Then I was alone with him on the platform. With my arm around his waist we made it slowly to the taxi stand. But back at the Warwick the desk clerk fixed us with a fishy eye, insisted he had not expected us back for several days and that all the rooms were taken. Again, no room at the inn. For nearly three hours that Sunday morning we taxied the nearly deserted streets of East Side Manhattan in search of public hospitality. But such was our physical state and unkempt appearance that not even the meanest of hotels would have us. Finally, at Scott's whispered suggestion, we fell back on one of his familiar ports in the days of other storms, Doctors Hospital. Somewhere along the way Scott had called his daughter Scottie at Vassar to meet him in the city. Now he was worried that she should find him in this condition. He asked me to intercept her at the Plaza. I was still new to the crossroads of New York, and that afternoon, particularly rattled. At any rate I waited for nearly three hours, in vain—at the *Savoy* Plaza on the opposite corner from Scott's Plaza. As a result I never met his daughter and have always felt unhappy about that mishap, just as I felt an innocent accessory to the crime in offering Scott champagne and deserting him for those few critical hours on arrival in New York, when there still might have been time to help him fight his demons. I plead innocent because no one had taken the trouble to spell out for me, until it was too late, the hard fact that Scott was an alcoholic.

He had asked me not to tell Sheilah Graham where he was. I tried to honor this for the better—or I should say worse—part of a day, but I had to meet her at the Elysée Hotel she had chosen near the Warwick, and once she knew he had not returned there she could guess where he was without my having to tell her. She said she would stay on to look after him and that I could fly back to the Coast.* Since that distant day, Sheilah and I have been as close to each other and as far from each other as two people can be. But no one who saw them together could ever question her devotion to Scott. Though she may

---

* This episode has been described with an inaccuracy that can only be ascribed to malice in Andrew Turnbull's biography, *Scott Fitzgerald*. Some of its errors regarding my association with Scott were inherited by Henry Dan Piper in *F. Scott Fitzgerald: A Critical Portrait*. Miss Graham and I, in a recent reunion after a long misunderstanding, reviewed the events as they are stated here.

have looked like a British music-hall lovely playing Florence Nightingale, she loved him and she nursed him and a week later he was strong enough to make the trip back to Hollywood. So ended what Malcolm Cowley had called "his biggest, saddest, most desperate spree."

When I limped back to town I was rehired for *Winter Carnival,* along with a new team consisting of a Dartmouth contemporary of mine and a middle-aged Stalinist with an affinity for good dependable hack work. But Scott continued to work on that battered scenario in a curious fashion. From time to time he would send me notes, helpful bits I might have forgotten (or failed to notice). "Don't forget to put in something about the student waiters at the eating clubs who lean over the shoulders of their fellow classmate they're serving, getting into intimate discussions with them about the events of the day, the 'cute babe' at the ski jump, etc." He also suggested that, playing on the theme of Dartmouth's origin as an eighteenth-century school for Indians, we begin with a prologue showing young squaws on snowshoes invading the log-cabin classroom to dance with the braves. "From there you could dissolve to the station for the arrival of the girls," Scott wrote, breaking one of those solemn commandments he had set up for himself in the confessional and reappraisal he had written for *Esquire:* "If you are young and you should write asking to see me and learn how to be a sombre literary man writing pieces upon the state of emotional exhaustion that often overtakes writers in their prime—if you should be so young and so fatuous as to do this, I would not do so much as acknowledge your letter, unless you were related to someone very rich and important indeed." And Scott had gone on to belabor his new-found asceticism or cynicism: "And if you were dying of starvation outside my window, I would . . . stick around till somebody raised a nickel to phone the ambulance, that is if I thought there would be any copy in it for me." And, he almost crowed, "I have now at last become a writer only."

But if the world is divided into givers and takers, Scott's

temperament assigned him to the former even if the realities of his "emotional exhaustion" urged his siding with the self-protective egoists. What could he gain from these further thoughts on *Winter Carnival?* If he had sent them directly to Walter Wanger, one might suspect that he was trying to make amends, and to curry favor with one of the powers of the industry. But against his own self-interest and the porcupine resolutions formed as he stepped warily over the threshold between the ages of thirty-nine and forty, he had taken precious time to send these notes directly to me, some of them extremely perceptive and even helpful, though not even Scott's loyalty to me and to a project that had cruelly defeated him could save our stricken film.

Winter Carnival turns up now and then on the Late Late Show, used by inveterate television viewers as a substitute for sleep. One evening recently, in a mood of masochism lined with curiosity, I forced my eyes to remain open if glazed through an entire screening. It is not really a film at all but an anthology of disparate concepts and obsessions. There is Walter Wanger's starring role for Ann Sheridan, throwing the drama out of focus. There's my radical college editor, the only thing I knew how to or wanted to write that season. Here and there, in the dialogue of the English professor and his ex-flame who gets off the train to find him on a sentimental impulse, you may even hear ever so faintly the voice of F. Scott Fitzgerald. Watching the film I found myself muttering, "That's *mine*. That's *his*. That's *theirs*." Did I call it an anthology? Belay that. It's a smörgasbord left overnight on the table of a pseudo-Swedish restaurant.

When the film was unhappily behind us, I saw Scott occasionally when he was living in Ventura Valley in Edward Everett Horton's guest house. He was not well, he was money-troubled, he was haunted by the illness of his wife, concerned about his daughter's financial support and intellectual development, and doing his best, which was sometimes his worst, to maintain a tranquil relationship with Sheilah. What most impressed me about him in this period of sober anxiety* was his irrepressibility, his capacity for enthusiasm. Even in the face of misfortune it simply was not in him to be the misanthropic, single-minded hermit crab he claimed to have become. No, even after crackup and pasting together, further crackups and repasting together, Scott was still too curious, too world-conscious, too people-enjoying, too much the wide-eyed enchanter from St. Paul ever to put into execution the rigid acerbity he had in desperation prescribed for himself. He must continue to be a writer, he had said, because that was his only way of life, "but I would cease any attempt to be a person—to be kind, just or generous . . . there was to be no more giving of myself."

This was the same Scott who three years later was sending me notes of encouragement and guidance on a film job that had humiliated and rejected him; and taking pride in the work of Nathanael West, whose *Miss Lonelyhearts* he had been among the first to recognize and herald, just as earlier he had taken the young Hemingway under his wing. There was something naïve, forever young, about this capacity for wonder, whether it was turned outward or inward.

The Scott Fitzgerald I knew had surprisingly little *side*. Despite those few unfortunate occasions when he had slipped off the tailgate and would feel impelled to name-drop that he was F. Scott Fitzgerald, he did not act the famous author. At forty-odd he still carried with him the ebullient twenty-year-old who dreamed of the hit first novel that would win him fame, fortune, and *the* girl. One day when I was chatting with Sheilah at the Horton house, he burst into the general conversation with: "I've just finished an awfully good story!" Then he was running up the stairs to fetch it and hurrying back to read it out loud to us. It was one of the Pat Hobby stories for *Esquire*. At their best they were second-drawer Fitzgerald, with a sharp

* There was another macabre spree to Havana with Zelda that spring, but Sheilah was devotedly discreet and I did not hear about it from her until much later. On most of my visits he was determinedly sober.

eye for Hollywood manners and an outrageously downgraded reflection of Scott's own adventures in that sunkist company town. Unfortunately this particular piece was third-drawer. But Scott read it with irresistible if somewhat embarrassing relish, and seemed boyishly pleased with our murmured, qualified praise.

Another afternoon I found him out in the sun reading a thick Karl Marx pamphlet, *The 14th Brumaire*. He was like an eager sociology student bucking for an A in Bunny Wilson's class in social consciousness. "I've got to examine all my characters in the light of their class relationships," Scott decided, an earnest forty-three-year-old sophomore discovering an exciting new course under a favorite professor who was overstimulating him. One of the qualities that had set Scott above his contemporaries as a novelist was his intuitive grasp of American history and its shifting social classes, and I honestly wondered whether Wilson or Marx or the two of them together could help him improve on it.

One evening around seven he dashed into my house unexpectedly just as I was leaving (and, as usual, late) for a dinner party. He was all aglow to discuss Spengler's *Decline of the West*. Had I read it? What did I think about it? Didn't it put Munich and the Czechoslovakian grab in the tragic perspective of moral history? I can see him standing there in the entrance hall full of animated talk, making Spengler sound like a new, hot writer who had just zoomed to the top of the bestseller list. I remember fixing my tie and saying, "Jesus, Scott, I'd love to talk to you but I'm already late as hell, I've *got* to go"—walking out on him for some urgent social engagement I can no longer recall, and feeling guilty about it, even then. There was something endearing and enduring about his rushing in to discuss on the run the decline of the Western world. He looked old but, in this way at least, he wasn't old at all. Despite our cross-country debacle and another brief relapse or two, my most lasting impressions are not of his drinking and falling but of his thinking and trying.

When I finally extricated myself from the celluloid coils in the late Spring of 1939, I went to see Scott, to tell him I was fed up with film writing after our bad, sad experience and was going East to find a house near Dartmouth and try to write a novel. I told him something of my plan for expanding the central character, Sammy Glick, with whom he was familiar from a couple of short stories he had read and liked. We talked a long time that day about the old, silent Hollywood of my youth and about my relationship with my father and the big studio he ran. We talked about my summer vacation trip to Russia and the fear of the major producers, a rather cohesive in-group in those days, that I would turn Bolshevik and disgrace the Industry. When I returned from Moscow to Hollywood with a beard and a well-lined copy of Bukharin's *Historical Materialism,* the solemn pronouncement had been, "Let him talk to Irving." Although my father would have outscored him on a comprehensive exam in English literature, there was only one Irving Thalberg. In a town, or rather a principality, that had developed almost overnight the ability to create myths for mass production, Irving Thalberg had been installed as a demigod, a crown prince in command of Taste and the more serious aspirations of Our World. Scott pressed me for details of my audience with Irving and our inner-circle discussion of the temptations and pitfalls of socialism. I described the small, grave man in the large, tasteful office who discussed my Russian experience quietly, in contrast to the other studio chiefs who were cussing me out to my father and loudly demanding some form of public punishment.

But Irving remained thoughtfully in character. In his opinion the sons of producers, who would one day assume their responsibilities in the Industry, should be curious about other systems of government. He thought, to paraphrase Bernard Shaw, that anyone who was not a socialist before he was thirty was a damned fool. And that anyone who remained a socialist after thirty was equally a fool. He hoped, he told me, that eventually I would recover from socialism and youthful rebellion and become a useful member of the local society. Meanwhile he would try to calm the more explosive and abusive of the Big Five who ruled our kingdom like caliphs.

Scott was fascinated by Thalberg's acceptance of his role as the Disraeli of this self-contained but far-reaching empire. He had known him socially in the twenties, had worked for him at M-G-M before our *Winter Carnival* debacle and seemed to believe in him totally. I admired Thalberg, but with many more reservations, due in part to his rivalry with my father and in part to a built-in skepticism of Hollywood exaltation. It seemed to me that Scott was temperamentally more worshipful than I was, or perhaps it is more accurate to say we worshiped at different altars. At any rate, he praised my decision to cut myself loose from my Hollywood moorings, he suggested that we keep in touch with each other, and he wished me luck.

I had to return to Hollywood from Vermont the following spring because my wife had convinced herself that the only place where babies could be born in perfect health was Southern California.

I called Scott to tell him I had finished my book and would use the next few months to cut and refine it, at which point I hoped he would read it. He assured me that he would and said that after a long hiatus so far as the studios were concerned, he was working for an independent producer on an adaptation of his own short story, *Babylon Revisited*. How little he was being paid for it, he said, was too embarrassing to tell me, but at least he was working on something of his own that he believed in. He had moved in from the Horton guest house in the Valley to a small but comfortable apartment in the building Sheilah had been living in, on Laurel, conveniently close to Schwab's Drugstore on Sunset Boulevard, which had become the gathering place for the "Strip" community in those more serene pre-hippie days. Scott looked wan and he said he had been ill but he seemed proud of the months he had accumulated on the wagon. One evening he dropped in (a rare occurrence now, as he had been eliminating his evenings out) and joined me in a game of darts in my basement study. His coordination was off so badly that other friends were ducking because he was throwing at right angles to the board. A couple of drop-in acquaintances wondered if he was drunk. He wasn't at all. He had been hanging on to that wagon for dear life. But his nervous system was slipping out of control like a worn-out gear. Not his mind, though. His mind was clear and sharp and determined. He left early that evening because he said he was trying to rise early these mornings, to work while his energy was still high.

Along with a number of other friends—Dorothy Parker, Bob Benchley, John O'Hara, John McClain—I greatly admired Scott during this period. A love of life was still beating a strong pulse in him, and although he was inclined to speak more harshly of Hollywood after a series of souring experiences, he retained a marvelous capacity for descending through many levels of hell without becoming pinch-souled and defeated.

When my daughter Victoria was born I called Scott from the hospital as he had asked me to, and he launched into a loving twenty-minute monologue I hesitate to paraphrase for fear of failing to do it justice. It developed like a novella from the mysterious moment of birth across the various, difficult thresholds to the out-of-the-nest-and-into-the-world age of the college graduate. In Vicky's honor, Scott said, he was going to change the name of the child in his film script of *Babylon Revisited* from Honoria (originally named for the Gerald Murphys' daughter) to Victoria. Years later, ironically, Lester Cowan, who had bought Scott's story *and* film adaptation for twenty-three hundred dollars, asked me to rewrite the screenplay. I read it and thought it astonishingly good just as it was. I have saved it in my files as a quiet little monument to Scott's screenwriting ability, and to the promise he kept to young Vicky. Years later, after Cowan had sold Scott's script to M-G-M for a hundred thousand dollars, a wildly distorted version turned out under the title of Elliot Paul's memoirs, *The Last Time I Saw Paris*. Mercifully, Scott was spared this further outrage at the hands of his disrespectful old employer, M-G-M. It was proof positive that the Hollywood system of using writers as assembly-line mechanics was colossally wasteful. And to underline the irony, one of the champions of assembly-line writing was Scott's Hollywood idol, Irving Thalberg.

Scott's gift to Vicky was to autograph a first edition of *Tender Is the Night* I had found in a secondhand bookstore for seventy-five cents. In a hand again steady he inscribed the book "For Victoria Schulberg—in memory of a three-day mountain-climbing trip with her illustrious father—who pulled me out of crevices into which I sank and away from avalanches—with affection to you both—F. Scott Fitzgerald—Beverly Hills—1940." This was sixteen months after our "mountain climbing," but the avalanche had branded us both, with ice instead of fire.

Scott's obsession with survival, passion for writing, and his nagging fascination with Hemingway prompted a memorable phone conversation in that final season of his life. He had just finished reading *For Whom the Bell Tolls*. After praising all the good things "that only Ernest can do that well, or do at all," he went into a long discussion of the celebrated sleeping-bag partner, Maria. "Ernest knows how man fights wars, blows bridges, holds out, surrenders, dies—he's really in the big league when it comes to men dying—not so good on women dying—in fact when it comes to women in general, I don't think Ernest has learned a single thing about women since he was a junior at Oak Park High School," Scott said, and *this* I remember exactly as if I had taped it or had the total recall I always had envied in O'Hara. For a long time, while I shifted the receiver from ear to ear and murmured an occasional "mmmm-hmmmm," Scott delivered an impromptu essay on Hemingway's shortcomings as a mature novelist. "With all that childishness, and that's what it is, boyish dreams of sexual glory, he's still so *right* when he's right," Scott said. "But his mind doesn't grow. To be attached to a popular lost cause like the Spanish Loyalists keeps him topical and lively. But I think Ernest's egocentricity keeps him from maturing. He sees and he feels and he can squeeze the last ounce of emotional truth from a physical action, an action involving moral choice—better than anybody we have. But he doesn't think enough. A great novelist has to do all the things Ernest does so well and also *think*." Scott was far more critical of *For Whom the Bell Tolls* than he ever admitted publicly. He felt a professional loyalty to his old friend that was hardly reciprocated. The curious malady that aborted so many great American careers that should have flowered to full maturity was, in Scott's opinion, catching up with his currently more famous and far more successful contemporary.

There was, in what Scott was saying, awe, envy, familiarity, inferiority, superiority, love and hate and pride and objectivity. I felt that evening—though he did not say so explicitly—that he believed he could be a better or more profound novelist than Hemingway, and yet there was Hemingway doing it, in the mainstream, moving along confidently with a popular, compelling subject of the moment, while Scott, as far as Hemingway and most others were concerned, seemed to be floundering, if not sinking, in a brackish backwater.

Scott's extended phone call—there were many more to other friends—was characteristic, symptomatic of his reaching out; if physical disability was beginning to make a recluse of him, he was still gregarious and outgoing and would reach for the phone. It was his nature. It was the way he gave and took and learned and lived, despite his mournful protestations that he must conserve all that was left of him for his work.

When I felt *What Makes Sammy Run?* was as right as I could get it, I called Scott to ask if I could send it over. He said he was eager to read it. I endured several days of nervous silence and then his phone call released me from the compression chamber where I had been waiting for his verdict. His voice brought marvelous news. Full of superlatives, he said the book was "absolutely fearless," that it was "fresh and original" and "by far the best thing ever done about Hollywood." Beyond his words, the tone of his voice sounded genuinely pleased and excited for me, and once again his unselfishness toward other writers came home to me strongly. Tired, sick, embattled, vain and proud and painfully conscious of his fall from fame and fortune and creative productivity, he seemed congenitally incapable of practicing the sour egoism he preached. At the end of the day I hurried over to his apartment. Occasionally when I am back in Hollywood I find myself turning off Sunset Boulevard and thinking about those visits. For perhaps half an hour Scott told me the things he liked best about *Sammy*. It was the first of its kind, he said, and that seemed to delight him. "You know, you've really caught the feeling of Hollywood," Scott said. "You've always talked it awfully well but I honestly wondered if you'd be able to get it down on paper." He volunteered to write Bennett Cerf a letter about it that could be used on the back of the jacket. He said he wanted to help me because I had written a book that would make me as *persona non grata* in Hollywood as Sinclair Lewis had been in Sauk Centre after *Main Street*. Except, he said, mine was even a braver choice because Sauk Centre had nothing more to offer Lewis the successful novelist while I would seem to be cutting myself off from the professional lifeline of film writing. It was then that I told Scott my father's reaction. B.P. had been strongly impressed by the manuscript and at the same time had asked me not to publish the book. He had fallen several perches in the pecking order and he was afraid this might adversely affect his own career. And furthermore he had asked me, "How will you live?"

"The trick," Scott said, "is to have such a success that they can't bury it. If it's a flop they can banish you. But if you have a critical and commercial success, you can live without them."

I didn't realize until a few moments later that Scott was probably talking as much about himself as he was about me. For it was then that he told me for the first time that he had been at work on a Hollywood novel of his own, had been for some time, but had not wanted to tell me for fear it would inhibit my own first try. He had been relieved, he admitted, to find that while both of our novels dealt with big studios and their bosses, our approaches were so entirely different that neither of them impinged on the other.

Now the questions and those long talks about Hollywood began to fall into place (though I was still in for some surprises). I began to realize, as I had with Red Lewis, that Scott's friendship had not been quite so altruistic as it had appeared. No writer's can be. Fitzgerald, like Lewis, for all his humanness, was a writer first, a human being second. This may not be the Golden Rule but it is the ink-pot or typewriter-ribbon rule. "All my life I've found myself taking mental notes, even about the things that were affecting me most painfully and most immediately," Scott had said to me. "I mean at the very moment when you're going through the worst of it some little cold spot in your brain is reminding you to describe it in case you ever need it for a story." Now I realized that he had been taking mental notes while I had paced up and down reminiscing about my Hollywood of pepper trees and self-made immigrants, of my father's baronial battles with Louie B. Mayer, of all the sharks and their pilot fish gulping down the innocent sardines in the celluloid sea. I couldn't wait to see what he had written. Scott said it was not far enough along yet but perhaps one day he would show me the outline and the opening chapters.

I felt then—and this is not hindsight, for I tried to describe these feelings for *The New Republic* a few months later—that while he was physically on the downgrade, he was creatively on the rise.

Early in December, 1940 I dropped in to say goodbye to Scott. I was headed East for the publication of my book and was thinking of settling across the river from Hanover to start another. Scott was in bed, reading a chapter of *The Last Tycoon* that his secretary had just transcribed. He said—although he had shown them only to his secretary and Sheilah and Max Perkins—that I could see the first few chapters, "which are still pretty rough." The shock of the opening lines is still keen to me:

"Though I haven't ever been on the screen I was brought up in pictures. Rudolph Valentino came to my fifth birthday party—I put this down only to indicate that even before the age of reason I was in a position to watch the wheels go 'round. . . . My father was in the picture business as another man might be in cotton or steel, and I took it tranquilly. . . ."

Many years have passed but whenever I open this book I still get the same queasy feeling. For those were practically my words (except that I had said it was Jackie Coogan who came to my birthday party when he was a bare-kneed child star). My first reaction was a flare of resentment. Scott had led me on. Scott had cheated me of a birthright. Every writer has, we always say, just so many stories, and here was one of my central experiences neatly typed into Scott's book. He saw the look on my face and he said, with the shy, apologetic toughness I've seen in many writers since, "I sort of combined you with my daughter Scottie for Cecilia [the novel's narrator, who goes from Hollywood to Bennington instead of to Dartmouth]. There'll be quite a few lines you'll recognize. I hope you won't mind."

At that moment I wasn't sure whether I did or not. I read on. Again and again I heard myself. There were many moments when Scott seemed to be telling his story directly through my eyes. There were my anecdotes, my observations of Hollywood personalities with whom I had been raised. It was almost as if I had written the book and then Scott had filtered it through his more tempered and sophisticated imagination. It is still the most uncanny experience I have ever had with another man's work. For although Monroe Stahr, the last tycoon, was Irving Thalberg ingeniously and romantically braided through the nature of Scott himself, he was also in many ways my own father, who had also run a great studio for many years and was a sensitive man of artistic temperament who fell or jumped or was toppled from the throne. Looking back on it thirty years later it is still a moment unlike any other I can remember. Scott had channeled off into his book some of my energy, some of my emotion and special insights into Hollywood. The sneak thief of vicarious experience that every writer has to be had taken possession of Scott—probably from our very first meeting. I wished, quite frankly, that I could call back some of the things I had told him. Now that they were imbedded in his book, to use them again would be a most curious form of plagiarism.

And yet as I read on I began to simmer down. As a first novelist who felt that Hollywood belonged to him by right of upbringing I might look on Scott as a poacher invading my hunting preserve. But as a young admirer, I had to admit that the central character was a figure entirely beyond my ken or grasp. Monroe Stahr had a sense of nobility and a sense of mission that promised us a tragedy. Although I found myself occasionally quoted verbatim, and flushed when I came across our Selznick producer's-blood family joke filched and rather carelessly tossed away, I was drawn to Scott's unique or baroque realism, and to Stahr's heroic approach to picture-making that I, in what might be called my critical or negative realism, had been unable to conceive.

When he showed me some pages on "Robinson"—a literal, verbal snapshot of our frenetic, profane, competent cutter and second-unit director on *Winter Carnival*—I laughed out loud. One of the private jokes of our trip had been to wonder who would put the colorful Lovey on paper first. "All writers are leeches," Scott said, as if he had to remind me. "They fatten on other people's blood." Lying there in bed, a ravaged old man of forty-four, he looked like a rather bloodless leech, but the blood coursed with a bright vitality in those opening chapters. It seemed to me he was more in control of himself and of his material than when he was writing *Tender* so beautifully between crackups and breakdowns. I had doubts about his climax, as indicated in the outline he showed me, for the murder of Stahr by Hollywood labor racketeers seemed unnecessarily lurid, and while labor thuggery was being introduced to Hollywood I doubted that our Bioffs and Brownes would go to the melodramatic extremes that Scott was suggesting; at the same time I told him I thought he was on his way to a fascinating book that could be his best, possibly combining the depth of *Tender* with the precision of *Gatsby*.

He was pleased. "It's coming well," he said. "Just a few pages a day, except for a spurt when I wake up with a little of my old pep. But at least it's *coming*." By the time I came back to Hollywood, he said, after my own book was published, he ought to have a completed first draft.

"Marvelous," I said, and then, kidding, "I'll bring champagne."

"Oh God, not this time!" He laughed. "This time I know—I've got no choice—I'm on the wagon forever, baby."

When I stopped off in New York on my way up to Dartmouth I dashed off a note to Scott thanking him for the enthusiastic send-off for *What Makes Sammy Run?* which I had just seen in print, with his letter reproduced in full on the back of the jacket, and telling him again what a beauty of a start I thought he had made on his *Tycoon*. It excited me to think that he was on his way back to a pre-eminence some wind-tossed critics and a fickle public, deceived by those shifting Seasons of Success, had deprived him of throughout the thirties.

A few days later I was having a drink at the Hanover Inn with Herb West, a professor of comparative literature and rare-book collector who had been one of the handful of faculty members to respond sympathetically to Scott's disintegration on our ill-starred field trip two years before. Terribly casually, assuming I already knew, he said, "Isn't it too bad about Scott Fitzgerald?"

I put down the Bloody Mary and went out into the bright, cold December and leaned against the Main Street side of the Inn. I saw the cars and the people and the lively Hanover scene, but only dimly. In this very Inn, on another winter day when he was dying (though I had been unaware of this), he had been pleased, almost childishly pleased, to hear of my admiration for *Tender Is the Night,* carrying with it the hope—which he had almost abandoned—that his work would live on into another generation. With the frightening detachment that was characteristic of him, Scott had said, "You know, I used to have a beautiful talent once, baby. It used to be a wonderful feeling to know it was there, and it isn't all gone yet. I think I have enough left to stretch out over two more novels . . ."

That's what I heard, Scott's own answer to *Isn't it too bad about Scott Fitzgerald?*, as I leaned against the walls of the building just outside the coffee shop where he and I had declined and fallen together, trying to write a movie while each of us was composing in his head a Hollywood novel. As an odd result of our *Winter Carnival* experience, the first thing we did in the wake of that storm was to begin our novels of the film industry. Young, strong, and relatively unencumbered, with a seemingly healthy wife, I had been able to write mine in a nine-month gulp. Scott must have begun at almost the same time but his work was interrupted by ill health and staggering economic and emotional responsibilities to support Zelda in the sanitarium and his daughter at Vassar, forcing him to put aside his book for film assignments whenever he could get them or writing a wearying stream of stories for *Esquire* at $250 a crack—binding him to a slick-magazine peonage when he needed every last ounce of time and energy to finish the ambitious novel he had projected.

Aware of what he was capable of doing, and having recently seen with my own eyes what he *was* doing, it was maddening to read later that day the smug, righteous and incredibly ignorant obits in *The New York Times* and the *Herald Tribune,* as well as the cruel nonsense of Westbrook Pegler. They simply treated Scott as a dodo who had outlived the era to which they categorically assigned him. To them he was still the Flaming Youth of the Foolish and Bankrupt Twenties, the bad little boy who never grew up. This was sentimental easy-think. It was the kind of snap judgment that he had been struggling against for the past ten years. And it was not only the daily press and cantankerous columnists that repeated this error, countering Scott's own myth with an "early success—late failure" myth of their own. The weekly magazines got into the act, and our scholars and critics, who should have known better, complacently, almost slavishly accepted the prefabricated formula of "the short candle already burnt out," that had shone brightly but briefly with *Gatsby* in 1925 and had then surrendered to darkness in the Crash of '29. But the truth was that Scott had lost only his prosperity and some of his confidence but, as he knew himself, never his talent. But the loss of his public, and the critical abuse or total neglect he received from books on the contemporary American novel, set up around him an economic and creative vacuum that tended to destroy him. The negative things that most journalists, critics, and scholars had to say about Scott Fitzgerald until the day of his death had quite literally shortened his life, had made it more difficult for him to earn the money with which to pursue his lonely quest for development as a novelist, had influenced the public and the publishers who failed to publish or republish his work, or failed to keep the old books in stock. *The Great Gatsby,* for an example, was dropped from The Modern Library, and Scott's plea to Bennett Cerf that *Tender Is the Night* be added to that illustrious list went unheeded, as did Scott's plea to his own publishers that they publish a collected edition of his works, that they reintroduce him to a new generation that barely knew his name. The Four Seasons of Success, indeed! In fifteen short years a household name, accepted as a bona-fide genius by T. S. Eliot and Gertrude Stein, by Edmund Wilson, Malcolm Cowley, and even the competitively admiring Ernest, is not so much as *mentioned* in a new book called *American Fiction.* Nor does *The Great Gatsby* or *Tender Is the Night* receive any mention at all in a hefty volume entitled encyclopedically *The Rise of the American Novel* appearing in 1948, on the very eve of the Fitzgerald Revival.

Thus do the "scholars" blow their little wind machines that create false or dry Seasons of Failure that follow or precede new Seasons of Success. These are our Kropotkins who blow up Goncharov at the expense of Dostoevski or who sweep

Melville or Jack London too quickly to the heights and then before they are respectably dead drag them down into the mud of oblivion or failure where they are left to fester and rot while awaiting their posthumous laurels. Almost everything written about Scott Fitzgerald in the weeks following his death reflected a thoughtless, destructive, and indecently hasty dismissal.

They had tried to bury Scott half a dozen times, but the irony of it all was that he was very much alive when he died. Emotionally, creatively, politically, he was as ready for the forties, the fifties, and the sixties, the Now Generation and the counter-culture, as any writer I have ever known. What a pity it was, what a waste that he was not permitted, was not encouraged, to carry out the plan that would have proved this.

In a memorial issue dedicated to Fitzgerald two months after his heart ran down and his luck ran out, *The New Republic* fought back with a group of eulogies from a few of his contemporaries like Dos Passos, John Peale Bishop and Glenway Westcott, from O'Hara, eight years his junior, who also had been rushed to the front on the strength of a single book and knew how heady was that wine, and from this writer, who was exactly a month away from his twenty-seventh birthday and the publication of his first novel. There were some splendid things said in that special issue on Fitzgerald. I quote from my own tribute because it brings you the personal response of a young man (now grown somewhat older) to an author he admired then exactly as he admires him today. For if asked to comment this very morning on the passing of F. Scott Fitzgerald, I believe I still would write:

"Despite the twin ironies that the best book Scott wrote in the twenties had nothing to do with flaming youth, while his most profound (if not his most perfect) work appeared toward the middle of the thirties, my generation thought of F. Scott Fitzgerald as an age rather than as a writer, and when the economic stroke of 1929 began to change the sheiks and flappers into unemployed boys or underpaid girls, we consciously and a little belligerently turned our backs on Fitzgerald. We turned our backs on many things."

It had been unfair, I suggested, for us to transfer our contempt for the frivolous waste of the twenties to the man who had somehow come to symbolize that waste when what he actually had been attempting to do was to describe the spirit of his time, understand it, distill it, and turn it into art.

Westbrook Pegler, in his typical hard-hat style in the *New York World-Telegram,* related the memory of Scott Fitzgerald to a "queer bunch of undisciplined and self-indulgent brats who are determined not to pull their weight in the boat and wanted the world to drop everything and sit down and bawl with them. A kick in the head and a clout over the scalp were more like their needing. . . ."

Well, a kick in the pants and a clout over the scalp to *you,* old square Peg. If I had to choose my boats, today as I did yesterday, I would continue to choose Mr. Fitzgerald's. And if he wanted to rest on the oars and catch his breath a moment, before beating on against the current, that would be all right, too.

When *The Last Tycoon* was published as an unfinished novel later in '41, with a foreword by Edmund Wilson, there was a trickle of renewed interest in Scott's work. The trickle became a modest stream in 1945 with the publication of *The Crack-up,* which stimulated new critical appraisals of his work. The winds were changing. Bleak winter was giving way to early spring. William Troy wrote a significant reappraisal for *Accent.* The critics and the scholars who had largely deserted him were slowly coming back.

There is something farcical about all this, something unjust and inevitable as well as belatedly encouraging. With the almost simultaneous publication of my novel, *The Disenchanted,* and Arthur Mizener's biography, *The Far Side of Paradise,* the floodgates were opened. Both books became best sellers and this one-two punch brought to Scott—one decade too late to spare him all that torment of the spirit, the mind, and the flesh

—the new generation of readers, admirers, and enthusiastic critics he had been hoping for in vain throughout the thirties. People would stop me on the street to say, "After reading your book I want to read Fitzgerald but I can't find any of his works in the bookstores." Or they would write me that they were going to the libraries to reread *Gatsby,* or the fine short stories or the seductive opening chapters of Scott's last, unfinished symphony.

After '51 everybody, it seemed as if everybody, was having second thoughts about Scott. Leslie Fiedler, Alfred Kazin, Richard Chase, and other literary opinion-makers were re-creating the legend. There was a scholarly book on *The Fictional Technique of Scott Fitzgerald.* Scribner's did for him in the fifties what they would not do for him in the thirties, brought out a collected edition of his books, with no less than ten titles in the classy Scribner's Library edition. "In America nothing fails like success," I had written as the epitaph to *The Disenchanted.* Leslie Fiedler added his own variation in a later essay: ". . . but of course the obverse is also true: among us, nothing succeeds like failure. We are, behind a show of the grossest success-worship, a nation that dreams of failure as a fulfillment. The Christian paradox of the defeated as victor haunts our post-Christian world. None of us seems *really* to believe in the succeeding of success, though we do not know how to escape from its trap; and it has become one of the functions of our writers to supply us with vicarious failures for our second-hand redemption."

After the collected edition (o Scribner's, where were you when he needed you?), came more full-scale biographies, came volumes of his letters, came worshipful and valuable scholars who set up a *Fitzgerald Newsletter,* eager to publish every random note Scott may have left on the back of an envelope. A second postwar generation and an Indochina-war generation had rediscovered Scott with as much enthusiasm as the first postwar generation had embraced him originally. The two additional novels he thought he had salvaged enough talent for undoubtedly would have reinforced his hold on our lasting rather than our faddist attention. He was so eminently, uniquely American in all his strengths and weaknesses that it is little wonder his life and work have encouraged an American mythology. He himself had been a prime mover in this god-making and god-smashing.

But behind, or rather inside, this myth of the tragic poet fallen from the great Ferris wheel of Success in America, lived old Scott, the Scott Fitzgerald I remember, the most beguiling adventurer I ever knew.

As a culture hero of the seventies—back in fashion, in season—"Did you *really* know Scott Fitzgerald?" incredulous students ask me—Scott Fitzgerald seems today on even firmer ground than he did in the cocksure twenties. "This is not a legend," Stephen Vincent Benét has written, "this is a reputation—and seen in perspective, it may well be one of the most secure reputations of our time."

Hey, Scott, where the hell are you? Can you hear us up there? I hope you made it to the far side of paradise, where there's plenty of time, security, writing supplies, helpful publishers, and constructive critics. I hope you're reading your notices. I hope you liked the tasteful job Scribner's did on the *Collected Works,* the new titles they've added from the unpublished manuscripts you left behind, the adulatory biographies, the way they're getting behind the classy paperback editions. You wouldn't believe it, baby, but they even made a *movie* about you and Sheilah. Yep, it turned out just as screwed up as *Winter Carnival.* That's showbiz, Scott baby, which is, as you know, interchangeable with bookbiz these days. You couldn't have got yourself arrested in 1941—well, maybe that's about all you could have done without help—but in 1971 you're a live item, a hot property—why, instead of begging for a thousand or so to finish *Tycoon,* you'd be getting advances in the hundreds of thousands.

It's all a matter of time, baby, as you always sensed. In the thirties, and in *your* thirties, all the critics, even on the establishment papers, became experts on the proletarian novel. You remember. One critic preferred Clara Weatherwax to William Faulkner because he said Bill's work was frivolous and trivial. Well, what are you gonna do? Anyway, twenty or thirty years too late is better than nothing, isn't it?

That's right, you could die laughing.

IV ✧ ✧ PEP WEST
Prince Myshkin in a Brooks Brothers Suit

"My books meet no need except my own, their circulation is practically private. . . . You know how difficult it is to go on making the effort and sacrifice necessary to produce a novel only to find nowhere any just understanding of what the book is about. . . ."

—EXCERPTS FROM WEST'S LETTERS TO SCOTT FITZGERALD AND GEORGE MILBURN

"Soon after the publication of his *Complete Works* in 1957 . . . West was not only attracting advanced-degree candidates in literature . . . but a wide public: his books have sold, in all editions, over a million copies, and have been translated into nearly a dozen languages."

—JAY MARTIN, *Nathanael West: The Art of His Life* (1970)

NATHANAEL WEST was one of the regulars who hung around the Stanley Rose Book Store thirty-five years ago. Stanley Rose wasn't one of the characters in West's little time-bomb of a Hollywood novel, *The Day of the Locust,* but he might have been. "Pep," as West was known to his friends, loved Stanley and though Stanley had his favorites among the writers who made his bookstore on Hollywood Boulevard their home away from home (Bill Saroyan was one, Bill Faulkner another, this habitué a third), we all had to concede that Pep enjoyed the highest perch in Stanley's aviary of rare literary birds. And what a collection they were. Wander in from Hollywood Boulevard—that Middle Western Main Street with its sad, exotic embellishments—and you would find yourself browsing and brooding with John O'Hara, Guy Endore, Scott Fitzgerald, Erskine Caldwell, Gene Fowler, John Fante, Jo Pagano, Aben Kandel, Dalton Trumbo, Dashiell Hammett, Jim Tully, Tess Slesinger, Sid Perelman, Dorothy Parker. Strolling into the back room you found congeniality in the art gallery where original Picassos, Klees, Brancusis, and the best of our local artists—Fletcher Martin and Hillaire Hiler—were being seen for the first time in Hollywood's brief and spastic history, your appreciation basted with orange wine, a beverage that Stanley Rose dispensed by the gallon. The flock of published writers who migrated to Hollywood to refill their larders against the long cold winters of the Depression inevitably found a home in Stanley Rose's hospitality corner. But of all that motley company that huddled together for warmth in the back room of Hollywood's equivalent of the Mermaid Tavern, Pep West was one of the special handful that Stanley enjoyed seeing after hours (such hours as Stanley kept). On the weekends they would go prowling together, and a more excellent guide into the netherworld that shadowed the bright corners of Sunset and Vine would have been hard to find. For Stanley Rose, as a free-booting Texan whose light of intelligence and sensitivity was hidden in a bushel of amorality, had access both to the offices of the stars and producers of the big studios, where he would peddle his best sellers and his nonsellers out of a carpet-bag, and to the back streets and after-hours joints of Holly-wood vice. Stanley Rose was as much at home with prostitutes and would-be gangsters as he was with the littérateurs. This curiosity about the widest possible range of human experience was one of the bonds between him and Pep, who seemed to take a sorrowful delight in lifting stones to study the human crawlers that burrowed into the muck. As we had learned from Pep's grotesque fictions, he took a bitterly comic, Swiftian view of life—we all seemed to be burrowing into the muck and hiding from the light under our protective stones, as far as Pep was concerned. And concerned he was, almost in a state of shock about the human condition, a shock he expressed brilliantly in his short, stylized novels but managed to hide in his every-day life by showing us a personality that was easygoing, accept-ing, considerate, gentle, and cautiously affectionate. Aside from the night-crawling, the cockfights, prizefights, and Gower Gulch nocturnalia that Pep was drawing on for his novel in progress, *The Day of the Locust,* he and Stanley had another hobby that amounted to a passion. They were both indefatigable hunters who seemed to work up much more intensity in the pursuit of doves and ducks than in the discussion of Proust and Faulkner. Stanley was a determined anti-intellectual who liked to pretend that he never read books at all and only ran a bookstore be-cause he happened to like some of the guys who wrote them. Pep's erudition was impressive—he was grounded in the English classics and the Russian masters and the French impressionists, symbolists, and surrealists who had inspired him to work a vein altogether different from any other writer of the twenties and thirties. But Pep was as naturally reserved as Bill Saroyan was irrepressibly bombastic. Sometimes in the midst of all that heated chatter and excited discussion in the back room, Pep would be so slow and quiet that outsiders would think he was stupid. Obviously he had earned his nickname the way fat boys come to be called "Skinny."

One evening a group of us were noisily discussing whether the ending of Hemingway's *To Have and Have Not* meant that Ernest was taking his first baby steps to the side of the social revolution which all of us, including Pep, accepted as the inevitable solution to mass unemployment at home and the fascist aggression abroad. In a corner, talking with quiet intensity together, were Bill Faulkner and Pep West. I edged over to eavesdrop, thinking I might glean some philosophical pearls from these two gifted pessimists. They were talking about guns. Not guns with which to counter the threatened violence of our local storm troopers, William Pelley's Silver Shirts and Victor McLaglen's Light Horse Cavalry. No, they were talking about shotguns with which they planned to hunt wild boar on Catalina Island. Aside from Stanley and Pep, I can't recall any other man in the writing business who leaned away from talk about books as determinedly as Faulkner. Hemingway affected the antiliterary attitude, but he had a penchant for talking about the writers he resented and thus could be led down the jungle path to literature. But like Faulkner, West and Rose were consistent in their resistance to discussion of books. "Read anything good lately?" a writer just in from New York had innocently asked Stanley Rose. "Me? I hate books!" "Then how come you run a bookstore?" " 'Cause I like to keep a joint where my pals c'n hang out," Stanley had explained.

Although Stanley obviously enjoyed his insistence that he never bothered to read the books he sold, he cast a benevolent eye on the literary types who ran up large charge accounts at the "club" and at Musso & Frank's, the friendly restaurant where needy writers could always eat for free simply by signing Stanley's name. Some very good writers took advantage of this permissiveness when they were "between assignments," which was the accepted euphemism for studio unemployment. Saroyan must have eaten thousands of dollars' worth on Stanley's tab, but unlike some other recipients of this informal Stanley Rose Fellowship, Bill didn't forget his benefactor: a few years later when he sold *The Human Comedy* to M-G-M he cut Stanley in for ten percent of the swag. Stanley didn't like people to talk about his largesse for fear he would be accused of being a patron of the arts. He insisted that he liked Saroyan because Bill was always ready to go gambling, and that he liked Faulkner for his readiness to drink sour-mash whiskey and for his know-how with a shotgun, and that he liked West mainly because Pep was always ready to go hunting. "Pep would rather hunt than write, hunt than eat, hunt than hump," is the way Stanley summed up his admiration for his mysterious friend.

It was Pep West who exposed Stanley Rose as a secret reader. "When hunting season is over, Stanley likes to make us think that he devotes his weekends to whiskey and women," Pep told me in the back room one evening. "But he'll hole up secretly and read half a dozen books between Friday and Monday. I've even seen him carry a book along on our hunting trips." Stanley swore that Pep was defaming his character. And in a sense he was, for Stanley's public character drew its vitality, if not validity, from his reputation as a hard-drinking, hard-cussing, hard-wenching, practically illiterate Texan.

What was Nathanael West like in those years (1936–40) when we gathered in Stanley's back-room art gallery, drank orange wine and talked politics, studio hassles, and life? In preparation for this remembrance I recently jotted down a free-association list of adjectives describing Pep: hulking, big, awkward, melancholy, sad, strange, detached, withdrawn, shy, friendly, warm, remote, secretive, shaggy, tweedy, gentle, sardonic, defensive, hurt, bitter, introspective, affectionate, lovable . . . To check my memory I phoned a survivor of the Stanley Rose days, who had worked in his shop as a young girl and is now one of Hollywood's most successful literary agents.

"What words come to mind when I think of Pep?" She

paused. "Sad. Everything about him was sad. Even his mustache was sad. And melancholy. Strange. Remote. Detached." I didn't prompt her. "And at the same time," she went on, "he was terribly warm and friendly, but in a strange, detached way. Oh, and gentle. I remember him as terribly gentle."

What made Pep West such a curiosity in the gregarious backroom world of Stanley Rose's was the emotional and artistic poise he achieved through detachment. The climate of Hollywood in the late thirties, like our jazz of the period, was hot rather than cool, reflecting the restless political temper of the country. The Hollywood Anti-Nazi League could rally all but a reactionary or fascist minority for a spirited boycott of a dinner honoring Hitler's pet photographer, Leni Riefenstahl. Movie stars were raising funds for the striking lettuce workers of Salinas. When André Malraux and Ernest Hemingway came to town to raise funds for the Spanish Loyalists in their struggle against Franco and his Axis supporters, the crusading authors outglamour-boyed Robert Taylor, Gary Cooper, and Cary Grant. Hollywood writers marched in the ranks of Harry Bridges' striking longshoremen and flocked to the Communist-oriented American Writers' Congress. Some of the more prominent even joined the Party itself, standing by their swimming pools with clenched fists, looking toward that "better world in birth" where beckoned that benign social engineer "Uncle Joe" Stalin. There were strike novels by the yard that were analyzed and appreciated with intense—if not profound—seriousness at fellow-traveling cocktail parties and secret cell meetings. Socialist realism, as exemplified by the works of Sholokhov and the pronouncements of the most recent Soviet Writers' Congress, was clearly the road to literary Nirvana.

How did the despairing novelist Nathanael West adapt to this insistent drive toward political art? Refusing to involve himself in any of the fashionable literary polemics of his day, he simply and quietly went his own route. In a time when it was noisily demanded of writers that they align themselves with "the progressive forces" in order to write "significantly," Pep

West was a fascinating anomaly. While he gave lip service and physical presence to the popular causes, he somehow remained a determined negativist in a world of literary boosterism. Aware of the absurdity of his age—but a full generation too early to be in the cultural swim—he stood in odd contrast to his Communist friends, who were really Marxist versions of Red Lewis's Chamber of Commerce types, conforming optimists who had faith that all our problems would be solved once the people got together and marched forward shoulder to shoulder toward the promised land of Stalinism. Pep's friends and comrades—for he was a guarded, ambiguous member of Hollywood's burgeoning Left—were not so different from the other evangelists who swarmed through Southern California. What we had, really, was just another kind of religion, with a Book, *Das Kapital,* a pair of Messiahs, Lenin and Stalin, and a Holy Land, the Union of Soviet Socialist Republics. There was nothing wrong with man, *per se,* our Marxist boosters assured us. It was only the system that was inhuman. All we had to do was overthrow the system—and American capitalism already seemed to be tottering!—and man's true nature, his innate goodness, would at last be free to express itself. Yes, the world was dark, clouded with mass unemployment, virulent fascism, and wars of aggression, nearly all of Pep's friends were saying. But once the People organize, free themselves of their false leaders and tyrants, and work for the greatest good for the greatest number, there will be peace on earth and the world will be transformed into a socialist paradise.

This was what Clara Weatherwax, the *New Masses* darling, was writing, and what Tillie Lerner, the Françoise Sagan of the movement, was saying, and it had become chapter and verse for a whole slew of proletarian novelists, Albert Maltz, Tom Boyd, Robert Cantwell, Jack Conroy, Grace Lumpkin . . . all people of talent and capable of individual feeling but whose work was overwhelmed by the popular social myth of *The People, Yes!* There was friendly coexistence between Pep West and the realistic proletarian writers, whose work he quietly or privately dismissed. He was strangely divided between a social life committed to positive political action and a creative life committed to alienation, a bone-deep negativism, a terrible (because so very real) sense of doom.

In those Depression years, when the Popular Front was our Alma Mater and Pater, it was a rare act of faith to swim upstream. Eight or nine of every ten critics were oriented to social realism. When it came to literary judgment, the *New Masses* and *The New York Times* were often surprisingly in sync. The same kind of critical thinking that clobbered Scott Fitzgerald for his affinity with wealth and decadence in *Tender Is the Night** had its knives out for West and his novels of grotesque or black humor that refused to pay proper obeisance to positive collective action. The same people who now welcome a James Purdy or a Jules Feiffer for their sense of detachment and alienation were belaboring West for these very values or perceptions thirty-five years ahead of their time. With notable exceptions, they had failed to recognize his earlier novel, *Miss Lonelyhearts,* published in 1933, as an elegant little classic, a prose poem of human suffering and self-delusion *in extremis.* It is, like its author, tragic, gentle, violent, melancholy, and strange. In an age of Boris Karloff pseudo-terror, it had real terror in it. In the decade of the clenched fist and the confident comrades it cried out, to readers who weren't there, "God pity us all—if there is a God."

This may sound overwrought, but only West's characters and content were overwrought; the whole was contained by the sure hand of the artist gifted with the unfamiliar quality of detachment-involvement. *Miss Lonelyhearts* is the rare five-leaf clover, the perfect short novel, as flawless as Fitzgerald's *The Great Gatsby,* as soul-disturbing as Mann's *Death in Venice,* as provocative a parable as Dostoevski's *Grand Inquisitor.* Happily this deeply unhappy book has survived the time-trapped critics and public that abused, neglected, or ignored

---

* "Dear Mr. Fitzgerald, you can't hide from a hurricane under a beach umbrella," one left-wing pundit wrote.

it. Though in fairness it should be acknowledged that while
Pep West, in the years that I knew him, had earned less than
eight hundred dollars from his three published novels, there
was an elite group of admirers able to recognize him as an original: Edmund Wilson, Malcolm Cowley, Scott Fitzgerald, Philip
Wylie, Josephine Herbst, Ezra Pound, William Carlos Williams,
and of course his brother-in-law, S. J. Perelman, devoted to
Pep both as man and as artist, whose faith in him never wavered despite a decade of professional rejection.

At Stanley Rose's, the mantle of failure settled on Pep's tall,
slightly drooping shoulders like the mantle of success. Each of
his three books had been memorable disasters. *The Dream
Life of Balso Snell* had been turned down by so many established publishing houses that it finally had to be privately
printed. Even then, Pep had told us with the kind of inverted,
bitter pride that was his trademark, it had not sold out its original five hundred copies. In fact, Pep still had a few around
his apartment that he would have been happy to unload. His
second book, *Miss Lonelyhearts,* might have had a fighting
chance, thanks to its public endorsement by William Carlos
Williams, Wilson, and a discerning handful. But his publisher
had gone into bankruptcy, dragging Pep's first *succès d'estime*
into that swamp of total economic neglect from which many
young and gifted novelists never extricate themselves. *A Cool
Million* was considered a letdown and a disappointment, even
by those who had warmed to *Miss Lonelyhearts*. And the fact
that it was a year ahead of Red Lewis's *It Can't Happen Here*
as a fictionalized projection of a fascist take-over in America
did nothing to help its sales, which were virtually nil. The book,
Pep said, enjoyed a brisk sale among Sid and Laura Perelman
and other members of his immediate family. It wasn't quite
that bad, but almost. Apparently right-wing critics had rejected
the book as too apocalyptic, not to mention apoplectic, while
the Left had dismissed it as too facetious and comic to be accepted as a serious work of antifascist fiction. Pep's work was
always falling between two stools. It was the story of his life.

But he seemed to accept it with a rueful smile as his artistic fate. I never heard him rage against his almost unmitigated misfortune. I never heard him openly envy more successful writers. He would simply go about his B-writer Hollywood chores with a kind of begrudging resignation, as if grateful for small favors such as the $250-a-week salary that would keep him together, buy him a second-hand wooden station wagon, and keep him in cigarette money while he salted away a few dollars for hunting trips and, with luck, a little serious writing time. The peaks of success and the sloughs of failure are much closer than they first appear, Pep seemed to understand. In America the two extremes are so outrageous in their demands that the victim of one or the other must call on profound resources, a tremendous second effort, if he is not to be swept away. Just as Scott Fitzgerald was sustained by his sense of craft, Pep was sustained by his sense of absurdity. If he had sold four or five thousand copies of his novels, if he had earned at least fifteen hundred dollars or so from each one, that might have qualified as legitimate American failure. A small, *respectable* sale. But Pep's flops, you might say, were as spectacular as Scott's hits. They were deeply etched in the American grain. There was something catatonic and bizarre about them. That may have been one of the reasons Scott and Pep were attracted to each other. Put West and Fitzgerald together and you have a rounded portrait of the artist as a young American strike-out victim and home-run hitter.

It had been painful and difficult for Scott Fitzgerald to adjust to his fall from grace, from his high perch as the critics' and the public's darling in the twenties to his years in the critical and public doghouse through the thirties. But for Pep there was nothing to fall from. He had never inhaled that intoxicating scent of success that had overcome Scott and overjoyed Bill Saroyan. He had breathed the foul air of neglect from the beginning, spiritually sustained by only a handful of discerning believers. His manner, more than anything he said, seemed to tell us that he knew his place: to be as unique and uncelebrated

in his time and his world as was Franz Kafka in the late nine-
teenth century of Middle Europe.

There is an interesting relationship between their work.
Kafka's unfinished effort to write about an America he could
only imagine (*Amerika*) might have been a dream novel of
West's. And yet, physically and culturally, the two men could
not have been more different. Kafka was a neurasthenic little
Jew from ghetto Europe; West (born Weinstein) was a big,
tweedy, Ivy League Jew from a New York family. Prosperous
until the Depression, when Kafka thought of guns he thought
of pogroms; to the Americanized Pep West of our leisure-loving,
sports-indulging culture, guns were an avocation, a hobby, and
a companion on the prowl for small game in the rolling hills of
Bucks County and the valleys of Lower California. Yet,
strangely, this widely separated pair shared a dark vision of
man in a frenzy of futility, like a beetle on its back. Man flails,
man gropes, man scrambles for identity, man sweats to pull
himself hand over hand toward the prize of dignity at the top
of the pole. But in the dizzy climb man falters, loses his grip,
slips and slides and tumbles in a grotesque acrobatic that becomes ever more ridiculous. You look at man and you can't
help laughing until you cry. That's how I read Franz Kafka
and Nathanael West.

On the strength of *Miss Lonelyhearts* and the other idio-
syncratic novels, West was an inside celebrity to most of us at
Stanley Rose's. Aware of the catastrophic publishing history
that lay behind him and the promise that lay ahead, nobody
faulted him for working as a scenarist of run-of-the-mill tear-
jerkers at Republic Studio, considered below the salt compared
to major dream factories like M-G-M and Paramount. Working
on his own stuff, he was respected as a meticulous craftsman
and he was rewriting and then rerewriting the small novel that
was taking form slowly and surely. It was to be *The Day of
the Locust*. Despite the fact that the combined sale of his last
three books could not equal the sale for a single day of *Gone
with the Wind,* his devoted little band of followers at Stanley's

were waiting patiently for the new novel. That is the salutary
thing about literary groups. They may become cloying. And
inevitably they become ingrown. But just as porpoises are known
to close in around and support an injured member of the school,
a literary group is able to give an unsung member enough attention and praise to make up for his outside or public neglect.
When Pep West walked into Stanley Rose's, publishing statis-
tics no longer counted. He was the equal of Faulkner and Saroyan and O'Hara and the other literary wheels who hung out in
the joint. When he entered the Stanley Rose Book Store he
wasn't a hack writer from Republic or a failed novelist from
New York, he was a figure. Every writer needs a Stanley
Rose Book Store, every American success and failure needs a
room that welcomes him honestly as an artist and as a man.

Elsewhere it has been written of West that after his lean
apprenticeship he was beginning to rise on the Hollywood
totem and that he might have developed into an "important"
screenwriter. But Pep had few illusions about the Hollywood
hand that fed him. Saroyan, who played an irrepressible Dr.
Pangloss to West's Martin in *Candide,* might look to the day
when mighty M-G-M would allow him to cast his Fresno Armenian dreams up there on the silver screen. But Pep did not
have that kind of ambition or appetite for the movies. Even
though his tender and savage nightmares might have made exciting offbeat films.*

"I don't mind doing those C movies at Republic," Pep told

* When *Miss Lonelyhearts* finally was brought to the screen it was downgraded to a "typical newspaper yarn," a creative abortion in the style of
Hollywood's rendering of Fitzgerald's *Babylon Revisited, Tender Is the
Night,* and other material beyond the ken of the studio dinosaurs. However, in today's climate, more congenial to West's humor of negation, his
work may stand a better chance. At this writing *The Day of the Locust* is
soon to be directed by John Schlesinger, of *Midnight Cowboy* fame. And
Terry Southern, who may be considered one of West's spiritual progeny,
is doing the film adaptation of *A Cool Million.* We seem to be on
the threshold of a Westian Cycle; any moment Pep's gallery of Calibans
will be writhing across the stage of Broadway musicals and television
spectaculars. Pep's posthumous summer season of success seems ready to
burst into full bloom. *Sic venit gloria.*

me in the back-room gallery over a glass of wine one evening, with that wry permissiveness that was so typical of him. "I watch my friends struggling to get their social messages into their million-dollar situation comedies and it seems to me it takes too much out of them—that is, if they hope to have anything left for their own work. The higher you get on the screenwriting ladder the more they expect of you. This way I can write, 'Pardner, when you say that, smile,' or 'You *dot dot dot* mean?' and it's relatively painless. At my studio they're so chintzy they'll shoot anything. And if you wrote it too good they wouldn't like it. This way I give them a fair day's work and can still concentrate on what I want to write for myself."

In his novels Pep may have been a fantasist (though his fantasies were dipped in the acid of reality) but as a novelist he did not indulge in any pipe dreams about the popular success of his novels. No runaway best sellers were expected to pour fourth from his writing desk. The armor he wore against failure would serve to ward off the black knights of success. At the same time, while a sense of hopelessness can be a reverse kind of spur, Pep allowed himself a dash or two of optimism to season his dish of woe. Our mutual editor, Saxe Commins, who had known Pep in the days of the Liveright-*Miss Lonelyhearts* debacle, was intrigued by *The Day of the Locust,* fascinated by its characters and their jaundiced locale, even though he thought it may have been too unrelievedly distasteful. He encouraged publisher Bennett Cerf to offer Pep an advance of five hundred dollars, a sum Pep was happy to settle on. It was Pep's hope that Random House would get behind his book and that it might be the first one to enjoy a respectable sale. Even if it did not bring him a windfall like O'Hara's *Appointment in Samarra* and Saroyan's *The Daring Young Man,* he thought he had a chance for the first time in his career to sell the first two editions of twenty-five hundred each and to make a couple of thousand bucks, not enough money to free him of his Hollywood indenture, but at least enough to encourage his money-minded publishers to believe they might have a potential economic winner in Nathanael West. That could lead to more generous advances that would eventually disenthrall him to work and live fully as the writer of fiction he wanted to be. A modest enough ambition, you may say, for a man of Pep's artistic credentials. He never asked to be Margaret Mitchell or even James M. Cain—just a slightly more solvent and better-selling Nathanael West.

Vividly I recall the afternoon the first advance copies of *The Day of the Locust* arrived at Stanley Rose's. It may seem irrelevant, but Pep, whose philosophic calm could be disturbed by unexpected things, was outraged at the color of the book jacket, a bright, garish red, and also by what he considered the cheap and hideous red cloth of the binding. "I'm going to kill that Bennett Cerf," he said, in one of his rare outbursts of verbal violence. "What a cheap, lousy-looking jacket! It spoils the whole thing! I'm ashamed for people to see it!" In vain did Stanley Rose and I, and other cronies, try to reassure Pep that the jacket and the binding were not the tragic failure they appeared to him. That particular spring day he was not to be consoled. It was, to him, a symbol of his publisher's neglect. From the shelves he drew other Random House books to compare their glossy packaging with the shabby job they had done on his. Twice before he had suffered with insolvent publishers. Now at last he had one that seemed to be flourishing, publishing Faulkner, Lewis, O'Neill, and a full team of superstars. And the way Random House stayed in the black, he bitterly divined, was by stinting on the stuff in which they had no faith. It was not the outside of a book that mattered, we tried to soothe him, but what was inside that would determine its future. Our words slid off Pep's back like the water from the ducks he loved to hunt. When I asked him to autograph the book for me he wrote fretfully, "For Budd—It can be used as a flag when the day comes! Affectionately—Pep West/April 17 '39."

Stanley Rose did his ruddy best to make a festival of the occasion. He built a proud little pyramid of the red-jacketed copies in the window. Undoubtedly his was the only bookstore in America to give this book its due. In fact, a more successful novelist whose book happened also to be coming out that week objected that his work was being shunted aside while Pep's, which could not expect one tenth the sale, was given star billing. But neither a more distinguished jacket nor a favored place in all the bookstore windows of America would have helped *The Day of the Locust* in 1939. Pep's premonition, spawned in the experience of failure, proved unfortunately accurate. The book failed to attract an advance sale, nor did the occasionally favorable review draw buyers to the bookstores. In the first months after pub date only half of the first printing of twenty-five hundred had been sold. Seeing no future or profit in the book, Random House did no advertising. The fact that this was a literary event was totally lost on a publishing world more attuned to John Marquand, Ellen Glasgow, and Margaret Kinnan Rawlings.

In a letter to Scott Fitzgerald, who had championed him consistently and unselfishly, Pep summed up the critical reaction: "So far the box score stands: Good reviews—fifteen percent, bad reviews—twenty-five percent, brutal personal attacks —sixty percent." Yet the book seemed to some of us at the time a worthy companion to *Miss Lonelyhearts,* an uncanny little novel, so irresistible in its wild daring and originality that not only did you not put it down, you are tempted to turn right back to page one and read it through again. Left-wing critics, including some of Pep's own Communist friends, complained that it focused only on what was vicious and depraved about Hollywood and that it was blind to the positive activity of "the progressive forces." And at the time, still under the influence of the comrades, although increasingly restive about their intellectual integrity, I thought Pep might have overfreaked his view of the film society. But with each rereading my social presumptions receded before the instinctive and insistent truths of that savage cry havoc of a book.

What a sad show for the critics and the readers that they were not there to greet it the first time around. To Pep's credit, he never quit. Like a runner lapped in a two-mile race, he sucked in his pride and kept going. It simply meant writing more movies and waiting a little longer. After all, he was only thirty-six. As a hack scenarist he was patiently working himself up the ladder. He almost never complained, like most of us, about the butchery performed on our scripts by "those ignoramuses in the front office," as we were wont to call producers. His attitude was not unlike that of a second banana in burlesque who accepts being clobbered by a rubber salami as all in a day's work. He maintained, or cultivated, you might say, a healthy streak of masochism that accepted failure as the inevitable dark lining of success. Given his bleak view of humanity and the society it created, a world he coldly despised even while being warmly fond of the human beings who were trapped in it, he might have shrugged off popular success as a gratuitous insult to his special intelligence. That was why I felt that Pep would be as immune to success as he had been to failure. Like his stoic hero, Lem Pitkin in the deadpan antifascist romp *A Cool Million,* Pep could lose an eye, all of his teeth, a leg, and his scalp, cheerfully-cheerlessly keep on plugging, and not be too surprised to find himself hailed—posthumously, of course—as the exalted and martyred hero of a new movement.

For personal reasons, as well as through my interest in Pep's progress, I remember the disappointing sale for *The Day of the Locust.* When I went East that spring to check in with Random House, pick up my $250 advance and report to Bennett Cerf that I was ready to retreat to Vermont and embark on my novel, Bennett—who would probably have described himself as a man of dollars and sense—cried out with considerable pain, "Oh no, not another Hollywood novel! The people who are interested in Hollywood don't read books. And vice versa. You know what happened with Pep's. It's a damned interesting little novel—Edmund Wilson likes it—but we'll be lucky if we get rid of fourteen hundred copies."

For contributing this risible and terrifying little masterpiece to our permanent library, Nathanael West earned the grand sum of five hundred dollars—or roughly what he received for one week of writing "They-went-that-a-way" dialogue for the movies. And Bennett complained—in extolling the virtues of low advances for novels about Hollywood—that Pep's royalties had not even earned back his five-hundred-dollar advance. The total gross of the book—said Cerf in the voice of the crucified—was a measly thirty-five hundred dollars, not enough to cover the cost of printing, binding, and distributing. And Pep was complaining, Bennett said, that Random House was not getting behind the book with advertising. Pep had even offered to share the expense in the hope of pushing the book into a second printing. Bennett Cerf was like a benevolent but patronizing and scolding parent. Authors, in his view, were like children begging for larger allowances or more attention. If a book sold fifty thousand, Bennett would tell you, the successful author would be put out because he was sure that with fuller advertising it would have sold another fifty thousand. And if a book sold only one thousand, the failed author would be convinced that the publisher had sabotaged his brainchild and that a little expeditious advertising and all-around support would have lifted it into the black.

It was true that for a couple of months Pep West behaved like any frustrated writer fretting over sales and his publisher's lack of initiative. Then he settled back into his familiar pattern of hack writing, hunting trips, left-wing Hollywood committee meetings scrupulously excluded from his fiction, and the patient procreation of novel number five. Amiable on the outside, undoubtedly seething on the inside, a quiescent volcano lending strength, beauty, and mystery to the sun-baked Hollywood landscape, he had mastered the art of living through the Dead Season of Failure.

In warming up to this assay into the times and tides of Pep West, I picked up *The Day of the Locust* and began to read through it again. It is always with a sense of trepidation that one approaches old loves. I remember what a sense of relief it was to find that I still loved *The Bridge and the Jungle* in the same fresh way I had when it first came to my hands in the middle thirties. Same with *Fontamara* and *Bread and Wine*. Traven and Silone get A's for abiding. I had reviewed Pep's novel for *The New York Times* years before, but how often have you reread books once adored that crumble in your hands on third or fourth reading? Was *The Day of the Locust* a mirage? What if it no longer enveloped me as it did when I first lived my way into it more than thirty years earlier?

No sweat, as our sons say these days. From the opening pages I was drawn back into this puke-green phantasmagoria of life in the lower depths of the house of horrors that becomes Pep's metaphor for Hollywood. There was the Westian boardinghouse, so true to the design of those stucco monstrosities north of Hollywood Boulevard, with its "pink Moorish columns which supported turnip-shaped lintels." There was the outrageous, arrogant dwarf, Abe Kusich, the local bookie—who was not quite the aberrant creature he seemed, since we all knew such a character, a fixture on the gaudy streets of Hollywood and at the Legion Stadium boxing matches on Friday nights. There was Faye Greener, who is all the teen-age voluptuaries who ever flung themselves at the studio gates. I related them to the hordes of Faye Greeners who used to live in the apartment house immediately facing the entrance to the Paramount Studio on narrow Marathon Street. An apartment houseful of high school beauties who seemed to have all come out on the same train from the same small town in the Middle West with the same empty hunger to be "discovered"—how deftly Pep rolled them all into one delicious, malicious bundle of fractured dreams. And Faye's old man, the ex-vaudevillian to end them all, reduced to selling silver polish door to door, for whom every strange hallway is a stage as he hams his way into the grave. His death scene, with his daughter indulging in narcissistic primping with her back to him, is like a realistic Hollywood scene refracted through the distortion mirrors of Pep West's mind. It is only one of a hilarious collection of madhatter vignettes that start with a laugh and end with a gasp that becomes a sob.

For what makes this book so special is Pep's absolutely original way of illuminating his dark canvas with lightning flashes of wild humor. Wild in the sense of savage. It may be no accident that Pep and his brother-in-law, Sid Perelman, were such intimate friends, for artistically there is a definite connection between them. Perelman is not just a *funny* funny man, a verbal magician who knows how to take sublime material and render it ridiculous; there runs through all his humor a savage rejection of human foibles. It is almost as if West's books were the works that S. J. Perelman might have written if he had turned his talents to the novel, as if Pep's art were the logical extension in a more profound form of the howlingly funny parodies and put-ons Sid has given us down the years. In West we find the true gallows humor, which so often seems forced and self-consciously sensational in the currently fashionable theater and in the novel and the theater of the absurd that West foreshadowed.

Just as in the thirties we had "premature antifascists," punished for their sins of anti-Nazism before Western society as a whole was ready to commit itself to a war for survival, so Nathanael West clearly was guilty of premature absurdism, premature pessimism, premature alienation, premature black comedy. In the irresistible search for literary continuity, one might point to Nathanael West as the American from whom derive Carson McCullers, Joseph Heller, John Hawkes, James Purdy, Thomas Pynchon, and other poets of perversity who employ the jocular to attack the jugular. He anticipated the style of Beckett and Ionescu. He is the spiritual father of *They Bombed in New Haven* and *Oh, Dad, Poor Dad, Mama's Hanging in the Closet and I'm Feeling So Sad*. It took the soul-shocked sixties and seventies to produce the kind of styled hysteria that Pep was limning for us thirty or forty years before that style was considered appropriate to anything more serious than Princeton Triangle shows.

As an innovator Pep was a perfectionist with an ingenious ability to combine pratfall comedy with impacted realism. *Locust* brings you a cockfight, for instance, that Hemingway could not have described more cleanly blow by blow. Every realistic detail in the book is impeccable. And the final scene, the orgiastic riot of rootless thousands drawn to a hyped-up Hollywood premiere, is realism, God help us, carried that one step beyond the limits of reality that transcends naturalism to achieve poetic insight.

Reacting to the mass hysteria of Pep's climax, I remembered as a young teen-ager driving to just such a World Premiere at Grauman's Chinese Theater as Pep described. (It became Kahn's Persian Palace in his updated Old Testament of an ending.) Our car was a resplendent chauffeur-driven limousine and I was staring through the window at the powerful arc lights and the thousands of screaming fans pressing against the ropes the police had set up to hold back the crowd from the movie stars and their escorts, who had become the gods and goddesses of this palm-tree Olympus. Suddenly a fat girl who looked about sixteen broke from the crowd, ducked under the rope and jumped onto our running board. "Who are you? Who are you?" she screamed into my face. "I'm nobody," I said. "Nobody." Clinging to the running board, in a paroxysm of self-abasement, she turned her head to the crowd and shouted, "He's nobody! Nobody! Just like us!" Then the loyal police moved in and dragged her roughly back into the crowd waiting to devour her.

All these everyday Hollywood happenings Pep observed, absorbed, and transmuted into the art of grotesque or neo-reality. The orgiastic crowd, loving you this moment, destroying you the next, is the very essence of Hollywood—as Hollywood may be the essence of our success-driven culture. How truly Pep has caught it and recorded it in acid. What a brainstorm of an ending—and yet how ineluctable—for the only Hollywood gothic novel.

Not long after the publication of this neglected book Pep

West courted and wed a marvelous girl, Eileen McKenney. She had that unmistakable Irish-colleen beauty and she was hearty, funny, warm, outgoing, constitutionally cheerful, and loving. Although her life had been shadowed by unhappy romances with several friends of mine who were talented but difficult men, there was no trace of emotional scars when she was with Pep. She seemed to find herself with him, just as he— to the surprise of all of us who had come to accept him as a loner—did with her. She seemed to be the ideal extrovert to match his introversion, and his friends were gladdened to note the change in him. One night in the spring of 1940 my young wife and I did the town with Pep and Eileen, hitting the jazz joints along Hollywood Boulevard and the Sunset Strip. Pep drank and sang and laughed and even accepted an impromptu jitterbug lesson from Eileen on the dance floor. We had never seen him so carefree and uninhibited. She seemed to be over-hauling his entire personality. A rival (and possibly jealous) writer was only half-joking when he speculated that the new Pep might get so happy that he would "lose that whole crazy, despairing thing" that set his work apart.

We will never know. Pep and Eileen were killed in an auto-mobile accident after only half a dozen months of the rare happily-ever-after kind of marriage. Pep was a notoriously absentminded and, if I remember correctly, myopic driver. The ghastly accident, just one day after the untimely death of Scott Fitzgerald, Pep's friend and long-time advocate, left all of us who knew them in a state of shock. It is my hunch that a more fulfilled, better-adjusted Pep West would have gone on to ever greater works, just as I thought Fitzgerald's most mature work might have been ahead of him, if only he could have hung on. But Scott was at the far edge of his physical resources. Pep was in his prime. One eye was focused on the tragedy of cornered modern man, the other on the comedy, with the double image blended in a rare, apocalyptic vision. What an uncanny shelf of books he might have given us in his next thirty-seven years!

But meanwhile, as we trudge or rock on toward our destiny,

we should be grateful for large pleasures in small packages—as the Book of Job is a small package and *Candide* is a small package, as are *A Season in Hell, Fontamara, Miss Lonelyhearts,* and *The Day of the Locust.* We can be grateful for the small but incomparable body of work bequeathed us by the satanic, God-searching genius of Nathanael West.

And I suppose we should be grateful too for the first Season of Success that came to Nathanael West a short generation too late for him to have been able to enjoy it. A new post-war public, aware of social idiocy and not limited by dogmatic social programs and an insistence on political solutions, was discovering in the writings of West a brilliant reflection of its own sense of chaos and helplessness in a world running more to madness than to reason. *The Complete Works of Nathanael West*, a milestone, was published in the late fifties. Recently a glowing and perceptive book by Jay Martin, *Nathanael West: The Art of His Life,* was published. Once again, as with the truncated career of Scott Fitzgerald, the trickle became a healthy stream became a flowing river became a roaring Niagara. In the frustrating, resolute time allotted their author, all of Pep's books together probably did not sell more than five thousand copies. Now, in the various editions and translations, the sale is well beyond a million. Pep, I know this sounds funny, but you made it, kid! After a mere thirty years you're one helluva popular success. Yes, Scott and Wilson and Cowley and Williams and your small cheering section in the back room of Stanley Rose's were right all the time. Crazy thing is, Pep, you would have been rich. You would have been up to your elbow patches in shotguns and the latest in wilderness stuff from Abercrombie & Fitch. You could have lived the life of the writer entirely devoted to your craft just the way you dreamed it and knew in your despairing, forbearing heart it would never be. And as for movies, instead of your doing *their* movies, they'd be doing *your* movies. Look at *Dr. Strangelove.* They say Stanley Kubrick and Terry Southern, a couple of talented scoffers, wrote it. That's a way-out Nathanael West Production if ever we saw one.

All of the other writers in this adventure into the topsy-turvy world of success and failure were figures who lived on the highs of bestsellerdom and who, sooner or later, came to rue it and to struggle for survival or regeneration. Of the six friends I have chosen in an effort to understand the American snydrome of failure in success, success in failure, only Pep West never knew a moment of the popular acclaim that swept over Red and Scott and Bill and the others we shall meet. And yet I feel that Pep belongs with this traumatized group. For now the meat of his failure becomes the myth of his success. It is a good myth, it is a true myth, it is a myth we should not begrudge, it is part of what makes us as a people vulnerable and steely, foolish and wise. The work of Nathanael West, savagely, comically, tragically original, has come into its own and stands on its own two feet, wearing the ridiculous Emmett Kelly shoes of the clown ready to kick you where it hurts. If, in America, nothing succeeds like failure, then Pep West is now our most notable example. One stares back into the past and sees him standing there in the back room of the Stanley Rose Book Store, with his shy, almost apologetic smile and his lumbering slouch, his pervasive gentleness making all of us wonder how he could write those violent and uncompromising attacks on the American soul. And then, thinking how quickly his approach, equally rejected by conservative and radical, was to become the style, virtually the language of our age, one hears, as in the last lines of *The Day of the Locust,* the screaming of the siren and we may say with Pep, "For some reason this made him laugh and he began to imitate the siren as loud as he could."

V .♦.♦ THOMAS HEGGEN
Taps at Reveille

"I've got eleven thousand fuggin dollars rolling in every week. Everybody in New York tells me I'm the hottest young writer in the country. How do I go on?"

—THOMAS HEGGEN, FOUR MONTHS AFTER THE FEBRUARY, 1948 BROADWAY OPENING OF *Mister Roberts*

THE INK ON THE TREATIES of World War II was hardly dry when literary folk began to wonder if there would be an outcropping of war novels to match or at least parallel the literature of carnage and conscience that gave us Dos Passos and Hemingway, e. e. cummings and the now forgotten but bitterly effective Tom Boyd. Would it be the established writers of the prewar era, like John Steinbeck and James T. Farrell? Or the younger men of the thirties—Irwin Shaw, Jerome Weidman? Or would the troops themselves throw up unknowns, as already they had produced their Bill Mauldin in the cartoon field? Was there to be a new generation gifted with the power to express its loathing of mass murder, mass suicide, mass boredom, in novels that might take their place alongside *Three Soldiers, A Farewell to Arms,* and *The Enormous Room?*

By the late summer of 1946 a positive answer to these questions came in the form of a slender, unassuming, but endearing fiction called *Mister Roberts.* This was a pocket-sized first novel by a twenty-five-year-old lieutenant on a Navy cargo ship in the backwashes of the Pacific far behind the combat area. Here the enemy was not the fanatical kamikazi pilot but just plain boredom and the rot of inactivity. "The Reluctant . . . carries food and trucks and dungarees and toothpaste and toilet paper," Heggen begins his book. "For the most part it stays on its regular run. From Tedium to Apathy and back; about five days each way. It makes an occasional trip to Monotony, and once it made a run all the way to Ennui, a distance of two thousand nautical miles from Tedium. . . ." The Reluctant has brought down no enemy planes, Heggen's easy style confesses, in fact has never seen any. Only once has the martial command, "Commence firing!" been heard on the soporific Tedium to

Apathy run when the benighted Captain mistook for an enemy periscope the protruding branch of a floating tree.

Out of such material young Mr. Heggen fashioned a narrative that barely met the accepted standard length for a novel, sixty thousand words. But, as it turned out, every one of those words was worth a five-dollar bill and, as time went on, possibly even a ten-dollar bill. For the modest, unheralded *Mister Roberts* became, in the autumn of 1946, that peculiarly American contribution to international letters, the runaway best seller, the Book of the Month, the blockbuster, the smasheroo. First it was read in tens of thousands, then hundreds of thousands, and eventually in various editions its sale would soar into the millions. In the swift and glorious progression of Ars Americana (when the "property" is "hot"), it was turned into a play by young Heggen and Broadway's sure-fire Joshua Logan, and there it was, lighting and thundering up the skies of '48 and rolling onward and upward toward Hollywood. The callow, neophyte novelist of twenty-five was now the flabbergasted twenty-eight-year-old golden boy engulfed in fame and fortune. With the innocence of the true amateur Tom Heggen had planted the seed of a small truth about our wartime backwater Navy. Only in America—as we all used to say before Harry Golden nabbed the copyright—could this tender sprout have proliferated and thrust itself skyward with that overnight assault on space and logic found only in fairy tales and that other kingdom of the farfetched, the American celebrity world.

It would have been difficult that season to single out any other American under thirty (or over, for that matter) who was enjoying or at least receiving the phenomenal quantity and quality of success being lavished on young Heggen. And so I was rather surprised when some mutual friends asked if I would mind if he came down to see me at my farm or whatever it was we were remodeling in Bucks County. Tom is a delightful, a perfectly marvelous person, and great, great fun, said the mutual friends. They were sure I'd be crazy about him. Why, I asked, with all the people he must be seeing in New York, did he particularly want to talk to me? Don't know exactly, they said, but he has asked us about it a number of times. He says he wants to talk to you. He says he's got something on his mind.

Thus it happened, a week or so later, that Thomas Heggen appeared at the farm. We could see at once that he was magnificently cast for his role as the Young Man of the Year. He was strikingly handsome, and eager in that appealing way of the outgoing Middle West, intense, even high-strung, but buoyant and ready to smile with you, and to seek out the conventional and absurd and to laugh out loud at it. In addition to the friends who openly adored him, he was accompanied by a handsome young lady of the theater. She was adoring him also, but rather silently, for Tom turned out to be a rather large, overflowing personality and his young lady obviously had resigned herself to an affectionate back seat. But with his girl, his witty and prosperous friends, his beamish, boyish smile emanating warmth, modesty, and achievement, Tom Heggen impressed me as the almost too-perfect prototype of the youthful success in America. What was in store for this young man with the world at his feet, as it had carpeted itself for another beautiful young man from Minnesota, Scott Fitzgerald, some twenty-five years earlier? Was *Mister Roberts* to be his *This Side of Paradise* (written the year Tom was born), and were his glory days to be shadowed by disaster? Or was this vibrant and apparently healthy young man embarked on a long and distinguished career in which book would build on book until a body of work rose and stood with Faulknerian authority?

If young Tom* had come in search of serious conversation, it was elusive in the first hours. We drank a happy succession of highballs and played a word game that was introduced as Tom's favorite, a game for the quick-thinking given to ribald wit. It was called *stink-pink*. They had been playing it all the

* In retrospect, I realize he was only five years my junior. But I felt a generation older.

way down from New York, our friends explained. And a writer-neighbor of mine, Heggen's host for the weekend, confided that stink-pink had become an obsession with Tom. "It's completely taken the place of conversation from the moment he arrived."

Stink-pink is a rhyming game. In its one-and-one-are-two stage, a stink-pink for a foul punch in boxing would be a low-blow. A stinky-pinky (both words, two syllables) for a holiday in Panama might be an Isthmus-Christmas. A questionable stinkeroo-pinkeroo that popped up early in the game (for Mussolini's horse) was "Italian-stallion." But these were the innocent ones. The real test was to plumb one's sexual vocabulary, crossing literacy with obscenity. In this department Tom Heggen proved himself to be, as Sam Goldwyn is said to have said, a clever genius. Over and over again I and others would be stumped. But Tom was bursting with bawdy brilliance. A stinky-pinky for a "tighter form of sodomy"— "snugger-bugger!" Another stinky-pinky for a polite young man in a crowded subway who feels himself pressed embarrassingly against an attractive young lady? "Pardon–hard-on." A stinkeroony-roo-pinkeroony-roo for "a girl with hot pants who looks for lovers in a cemetery" (protested because its rhyme scheme left something to be desired), "nymphomaniac-agrophiliac." Well, let us not abuse a dying horse. By now you get the idea. What is more difficult to convey is Tom Heggen's compulsive fascination with this game. Probably out of self-defense, because my mind moves like a walrus out of water when it comes to mental games, I began to tire of stink-pink and to wonder if Tom was ever going to escape from this escape from conversation. What had he really come down to talk about? I grew impatiently curious.

Meanwhile, we were carried along on our highballs. The evening seemed destined to go the way of so many pleasantly babbling social gatherings, those eight-hour nights of semi-innocent merriment from which you wake with the worst kind of hangover, the old regret that begins and ends with "Lord,

Lord, where did that evening go?" At last, around midnight, there was a crack in this mirthful Siegfried Line. Rhymesters were rhymed out; laughter drained from seemingly inexhaustible Falstaffs, and the moment had come to introduce another subject. A current *Time* magazine book review was the opener and apparently this touched an open Heggen nerve. We shared a loathing for a particularly obnoxious *Time* practice of using juxtaposed pictures and snide captions trailing off into suggestive dots to stab if not assassinate public characters not on *Time*'s approved list. Once more Tom's memory was prodigious, and somewhat to my dismay this too became a contest of memory and wit with Tom able to cite a seemingly endless array of *Time* pictures and their accompanying, slyly offensive captions. He despised *Time* with an enthusiasm that made my own criticism seem pallid, and while the demonstration proved again the keenness and sophistication of his mind (as if a penetrating Middle Western intelligence had taken on rather quickly a brilliant Eastern sheen), I began to feel that his excitement for this new sport of *Time*-baiting was another way of avoiding whatever it was he really had come to say.

By this time five or six hours had passed in a kind of manic congeniality which did accomplish one purpose. The intensity turned the hours into much longer units of time that might have been weeks, months, or even years, and when the grandfather clock struck one, I said, "Tom, why don't we find ourselves a corner, set a bottle down between us, and *talk*." And so, finally, we did. Then for the first time Tom fell silent. He drank and frowned into his glass. Across the room in another corner sat his actress friend, ostentatiously quiet. His adoring friends were Leaving Us Alone. Occasionally, they would look over at him approvingly or appraisingly.

"Well, I guess you know why I picked you out," Tom began.

No, I said, I wasn't sure.

"Because when you were just about my age you went through something like this. I mean one hell of a big effing overnight first-novel success."

He meant *What Makes Sammy Run?*, which I had begun writing when I was twenty-five and published when I was twenty-seven.

"You see, that's what I mean, we were just about the same age," he said.

"But wait a minute, Tom. I had a first-novel success, sure. But I wouldn't compare it to *Mister Roberts*. I mean even if it was a best seller and caused quite a splash, it wasn't the Book of the Month and it didn't go on and become a hit play* and the Hollywood studios weren't falling over themselves to buy it for six fat figures. In fact, they were falling over themselves to avoid it."

"It doesn't matter," Tom said, impatiently, "it was big enough. So the book clubs didn't take it and it wasn't a play and the movies were afraid of it. Just the same, it changed your life, didn't it? I mean overnight you were famous and when you came into '21' Mac Kriendler knew you, and Walter Winchell called you the word-magician and famous people you had never met dropped you notes inviting you to their fancy sit-down dinners? And everybody had something they wanted you to do, to write their life stories or to read their unpublished novel or to advise their genius children as to how to become novelists, or else they were in urgent need of money they felt you were singularly equipped to loan them? And acquaintances hung over your table and acted like old friends and your genuine old friends asked you on five minutes' notice to have dinner with them and when you said alas you already had a date but how about next Tuesday, they said, 'Don't bother— people told us you had begun high-hatting your old friends but we wouldn't have believed it if we hadn't heard it for ourselves. Now we know'? Your pre-success friends hated you and the more you tried to please them and prove you're still the old true-blue Budd or in my case the Tom of the Fort Dodge days, the Oklahoma A. & M. days, or even the Chappaqua *Reader's*

---

* *Sammy* finally came to Broadway as a musical in 1964, running 515 performances.

Digest or Navy days, the more they're convinced that you're patronizing them? I mean the whole crazy complex of it! Now, didn't all that happen to you?"

Over several additional highballs we commiserated with each other. It was tough-t, all right. This Instant Success, one quick, heaping spoonful and you've got it made, was something more than a poor put-upon freshman novelist best seller could bear. Yes, I admitted, all those things that he was charging against a success-happy society had happened to me and to many others I knew. And the phenomena had not the slightest thing to do with literature or the writing of a novel but in the great American Supermarkets of Bestsellerdom they were things that existed and had to be borne as the slings and arrows of a raging fortune.

As Tom described this onslaught of fame and confusion, personal memories of my own middle twenties were flowing back: John O'Hara, on reading my manuscript, saying rather mysteriously, "If I were you I'd start to learn a foreign language," and, on being asked to spell this one out, explaining, "You don't realize it yet, but you are on the verge of a surprising success, and if you are in the middle of something new that you're not quite able to cope with, something beyond your immediate control, it will help you keep your perspective." And sitting with Bennett Cerf in "21" when an established celebrity came over to ask my publisher, "How's he taking it?" as if it had just been discovered that I had terminal cancer or had just been nominated for the presidency of the United States. I had been "taking it," I told Tom, a good deal better than this inquisitor who needed to make a mountain of my lively little molehill. Most people come over, we agreed, not because they are in love with your work (though there is always a smattering of these and it is amazing how quickly you can spot them); no, they hover over your filet or your roast-beef hash because they are in love with success for success' sake, the opposite end of the spectrum from the art-for-art's-sake crowd.

"Do you know how much money I'm making?" Tom broke

in on our spontaneous editorial. "Eleven thousand dollars a week! From the book, the play, from everything coming in, eleven thousand fucking dollars a week! I've hit the three bars on the dollar machine. I've got so much money, it's—well, it's like drowning in money." He sounded not at all like a swaggerer or gloater. It sounded more like a cry of protest or panic from a swimmer struggling against the undertow.

Of course I hadn't made anything like his *Mister Roberts* money, I told Tom, and so I hadn't really faced his problem.

"But I know you did," Tom insisted. "I know you did."

"Don't try to drag me into your gold-plated beartrap."

"Gold-plated beartrap." Tom seemed oddly pleased with the phrase. "You see, if you hadn't been caught in it yourself, the image wouldn't have come to you so fast. Even if you made fifty thousand instead of half a million—it's not the total sum, it's the creative conditions for the second book that's comparable. The dough rolling in is just a symbol of what happened to you. That's what I came down here to ask you. That's what I've got to find out:

"How do you go on?"

Again, each one's set of circumstances, of creative conditions, is peculiar to himself, I argued. For instance, I went back to my writing base near Dartmouth College, was given a little office in Baker Library, and started on a second novel. Then Life poked its big fist through the roof and tossed me around. My infant daughter's inner-ear infection convinced my wife that we should return to Southern California, and whether or not you can't go home again, damn it I *was* home again, and against my will; there was marital trouble out there that sent me off to Mexico where I roamed around and worked for some Mexican film companies and learned something about pre-Columbian figurines from Covarrubias and drank too much tequila and admired the Indians while waiting for my commission in the Navy. Then the service, O.S.S., a second marriage, a tour of duty in Europe, an assignment to the Nuremberg trials, so that when I finally managed to sit down to the second novel on this dirt-road drafty and elegant dream house in Bucks County it was four years and a full life later. "You see," I wound up this little guided tour, "different man, different book, different problem."

"But at least after all those things, a divorce, a war, another marriage, more children"—Tom held on to *the* question—"you did Go On." (That's the way he made it sound.) "You finished another novel and it was also a best seller and you sold that one to the movies and now you're getting ready for your third novel. That's what I've got to find out. How do you Go On?"

Tom shook his handsome, keenly intelligent, and troubled head and poured himself another drink. "I know I keep asking that, but honest to God here's what I keep going through. I know it's time to write another book. My conscience keeps pounding that at me. So I get up in the morning, pretty late in the morning most of the time, because I've probably been out somewhere and drunk too much and was up too late but hoping to knock myself out so I could sleep—I have a hell of a time getting to sleep—well anyway, I get up and I roll a piece of paper into the typewriter and six, eight, ten hours later, it's still blank, nothing, not a single goddamn word all day, and day after day. That's why I keep asking, How do I go on?"

"I should think the first thing to do is to get yourself banked down," I said. I had been applying myself to the mysteries of a coal furnace and had begun to learn something about less spectacular but more durable fires. "Try to tell yourself, okay, I've written a book, I even think it's a good book, but it's still a little book, a nice, little book. In England or in France it probably would be considered a good, modest, promising beginning. We're glad he's with us, they'd probably say. We hope with the third book, the fifth book, and so on, that his stature will gradually mature." This was a few years before the English and French began to have their own nine-day wonders. "In that sort of critical climate you would have a chance for natural, unselfconscious growth."

"Now wait a minute, I'm not fooling myself," Tom broke

in. "Don't you think I realize it's only a small book, a fairly promising beginning and all that stuff. But just the same—"

"In other words, in spite of your own inner sense of values, you're caught up, trapped, in the great American multiplication table?" I asked. "It isn't one and one and one, it's one times two times three times four . . . each time out you've got to top yourself. If you don't, if you falter, if your second work is a letdown, a disappointment, a failure or even a modest instead of a whopping success, you're afraid it would be doubly, triply, quadruply a failure because it will be judged not for its own worth or meaning but against the skyrocket triumph of *Mister Roberts*."

"That's it," Tom said. "I hate to admit it but I do stare at that blank piece of paper and I suddenly tense up and think, Christ, what if I can never do it again? What if it was just a fluke, a neat little war experience that fell into my lap? What if I can never write another *Mister Roberts* again?"

"Remember what we said a little while back, it was never anything more than a nice, small book," I said. "The writing in it was solid and the experience you surrounded was real. But it was merely a beginning. In five years you may look back on it as a pleasantly youthful effort. Like the apprentice, pre-*Main Street* novels of Sinclair Lewis.

"Or take it from the other end. Let's say, Okay, *Mister Roberts* is *Moby-Dick* and *War and Peace* and *The Great Gatsby* and *Look Homeward, Angel* all rolled into one great masterwork. Let's say you'll never do anything quite so good or nearly so good again. So what? Whoever said that a writer's life should be like a steeply and rapidly ascending escalator? That's where the good old American drive of *can-you-top-this?* collides with the less competitive, less material creative urge. You might say that Somerset Maugham had the *Mister Roberts* problem. At least while he was still a young man, after two abortive, totally forgotten efforts, he hit it big with *Of Human Bondage*. Did he commit literary or lesser forms of hara-kiri because he could never equal that fuller, autobiographical work? Hell no, he went on, achieving *Cakes and Ale* and other delightful jobs along with some crafty potboilers. But he went on, enjoying his work and giving enjoyment to others and sometimes better than that because if you'll forgive the awful pun, he refused to be Of Human Bondaged.

"He was wise enough to realize early that a writer's career is not an escalator or a ladder or a palm tree to be monkey-climbed hand over hand. A writer, if he keeps on writing, is a mountain range. Look at any mountain range. Does it worry because every peak isn't Mount Whitney or that its own Whitney doesn't mount to Everest? No, it says, I am a mountain range, I go up, I go down, I level off, I drop and even fall away, then I pause and rise again, jagged, uneven, under no pressure to produce rise on top of rise on top of rise like a geological stairway to the skies. But when you look at me from one end to the other, I am a mountain range. I thrust my imperfect ranging form up above sea level and throw some sort of shadow against the sky. Tom, it may sound silly, or what is even worse, grandiose, but try to start thinking of yourself as a mountain range and you've got the battle half won."

"That's good," Tom said. "So if I dip below my present level but go on ranging . . . By God, I think that might be helpful!" He rose, paced energetically and filled both our glasses. "But I've got another problem, Mr. Anthony. I've been a little ashamed to talk about it to anybody but my psychiatrist. You see, it was a terrific experience working with Josh on the play. It's hard to explain, but he's so brilliant, so dynamic, he makes the work so exciting and, well, intimate, that it becomes a whole, complete world in itself. And I found that working with him was so stimulating, satisfying and just plain damn fun, that now this begins to worry me too—can I work without him, without feeling dependent on him? Creatively, I hate to admit this but I'm not sure I'll ever feel completely whole without Josh."

"Tom, you could look at it this way," I argued. "Josh Logan does have a kind of brilliant fever around him, it's the aura you associate with genius and yet the paradox is that Josh is much more of a craftsman than a genius. He's got the showmanship and the know-how and the sure hand, no matter how wild and unpredictable and fascinating he may be as a personal friend. I'm sure you could learn a helluva lot from him about fashioning your play and pleasing the bejesus out of the public with it. But when you dig back to the roots, Tom, there wasn't really any comparison between the book *Roberts* and the Broadway hit. It seems to me the book was better, simpler, truer. So you don't really need Josh, bright and show-wise and marvelously helpful as he is. It was you who wrote the real, original *Mister Roberts*. And I'm sure Josh Logan would be the first to admit it. And there's more where that came from, whether better, worse, half better, half worse, who the hell cares?

"Just relax and work hard but easy. Not even Bobby Jones could beat 'em all, and there was the day when not even Man o' War was the fastest horse on the track and all this horseshit about Ernest Hemingway being the heavyweight champion writer is crap that belongs more to the American competitive mania than to the world of art. Hemingway is wonderful, don't get me wrong, but the columnists, possibly aided and abetted by the Old Man himself, built him into a combination of Joe Louis and Jesus Christ."

Tom agreed. "We don't seem to be satisfied with a circle of three or four fine writers. We have to rate them best, second best, third, et cetera, like movie stars."

"Tom, if I were you I'd take myself out of all that. I mean, get out of the rat race. The best-seller lists and the Books of the Month and the press agentry and the money that just says 'fifty' for fifty thousand dollars, or 'two and a half' for two hundred and fifty thousand and all the rest of the hoopla that tosses young novelists into the same pot with the favorite pinups and the favorite brands.

"By God, Tom," I went on, because he had put me on and I thought maybe I had a flash that would be constructive and not just the same old self-satisfying drinking talk, "I know what you should do. Forget about the second book out-Robertsing

Mister R, or any of that stuff. Take your lousy eleven thousand dollars a week and get on a boat, go around the world, take a year off, take two years off, go ashore and wander around strange far-off places where you will be amazed how much they never heard of *Mister Roberts*. Look into the faces of the people who wouldn't know Tom Heggen from Tom Dewey and couldn't care less about either one, the people who are struggling through their whole life without knowing that there is a mink trap called '21'. Try to explain to *them* that you are suffering with a terrible problem, how to write a second book that will surpass the first one that made you rich and famous. In other words, Tom, get out of New York. Get out of all the New Yorks. And if you cannot go home again to Fort Dodge or Minneapolis, go home to yourself, wherever the hell you find yourself, which can be Ceylon, or La Paz, or, if you are strong enough, even Newtown, Pennsylvania. And take notes, keep a diary, not a self-conscious, have-to-write-immortal-prose-every-day diary but just an informal jotting of what you see and hear and feel and think. Maybe a book will come out of it, maybe not; just think of it as something that holds and heightened the pleasures of the trip."

"Budd, that's it! That's it!" he said.

"People will tell you you're running away. Bullshit. Just because your publisher is set up in New York and your play is running in New York and the circle you now happen to move in revolves around New York—none of that makes you a New Yorker. New York is just your marketplace. Every so often you bring your goods there. When you sell them at a good price you stay over for the fiesta. What I mean is"—I confess I was thinking of my success-ridden author in the projected *Disenchanted*—"cease to be whirled about."

Because talking and drinking is a much longer way around than writing and reading, this is a capsule version of what we said. We went on for hours. In fact we were still batting this around when Tom looked out the window and said, "My God—

we've talked ourselves out of the night and into tomorrow. It's a new deck. We've got a new day."

"I'd like to come down and do this again," he said as we walked out into the fresh morning. "Cease to be whirled about —mountain range—slow boat to China—I'm going to hang on to that."

"Come down anytime," I said. "Just call and say you're on your way." We embraced.

I never really talked to Tom Heggen again. A month or so later in a crowded, fashionable New York saloon I happened to see him again. Tom was with a group of friends, drinking and laughing it up in his merry and infectious style. I had the feeling that he still had at least one foot caught in that gold-plated beartrap, and he more or less confirmed this apprehension.

"Still got the old blank-page trouble," he said, putting it lightly, as was his way until he peeled himself back to the serious core. "But I've been thinking about what you told me. I may sneak down and see you next week." And he turned back to his table of the famous and the witty who had become his friends.

So I never knew Tom Heggen as I had had a chance to know Sinclair Lewis, Scott Fitzgerald, John O'Hara, Nathanael West, Dorothy Parker, William Saroyan, Charles Jackson, and some of our other celebrated American writers. But when I picked up the paper soon after our casual encounter in New York and read that he was dead, I felt as if someone had blackjacked me at the back of my neck.

His housekeeper had found him dead in a bathtub filled with water. Apparently he had been out late the night before and had sought a hot bath as a refuge from jumpy nerves. It was not suicide, at least not according to the official verdict. Tom's psychiatrist would say only that "the playwright has been mentally depressed and suffering from insomnia." There were half a dozen bottles of barbiturates in the medicine chest and even the whispered suggestion from a close friend that a razor blade had been found at the bottom of the tub.

These sordid details of Tom's premature obituary are not put down for the sake of innuendo or posthumous gossip, only as painful symbols of a fevered talent snuffed out almost in its infancy. The terrible, short-lived end of Tom Heggen might not have been suicide in its extreme, criminal, sinful, or psychotic form. And yet, once I began to absorb the shock of his death, the manner of his leaving did not surprise me as much as it would have if I had not been haunted with the memory of his anguished question, "How do you Go On?"

In a work devoted to the Four Seasons of Success as seen through personal encounters with a half-dozen writers of literary triumphs whose years of birth were 1885, 1896, 1902, 1903, 1908, and 1919, there may be a sinister temptation to see Tom's tragedy in terms of the master theme that in America nothing fails like success. Was not Tom's astonishing success the most spectacular of our failures, a frenetic, speeded-up version of the ravages of fame that brought Sinclair Lewis down in his fifties, wounded Saroyan before he was forty, and forced Scott Fitzgerald to sound the comeback tone of an old man when he was only thirty-eight? I hesitate to press my case, partly because, alas, it is too painfully strong a case to have to press. But partly, too, because Tom Heggen was a victim of so many things that it would be a shame to make him also a victim of oversimplification.

The demons of success, the twin demons of how-do-I-top-myself/how-do-I-go-on? that frenzied and frightened Tom Heggen, were not alone in driving him to desperation. Undoubtedly, poor Tom was pursued by more personal demons. There were emotional confusions, exposed ganglia attached to not one but three or four very different persons whose love for him or lack of it failed him; in their wake lay terrible guilts and frustrations.

In his short history, the rush of adulation had not yet produced its peculiarly American counterthrust—the curious, creative faltering of middle age accompanied by smoldering neglect. In Tom's case it almost seemed as if he did not have the patience to wait for this American malaise to overcome him. The way some men daydream their success, he was prematurely or immaturely nightmaring and anticipating his failure. And so, with his one small book and his brief, triumphant, and unhappy life, Tom Heggen takes his place in the drear memorial gallery of American literary heroes who enter with a bang and depart with a sigh for their lost promise and for the spiritual IOU's of their youth that must lie forever unredeemed in the hope chest of our brilliant, powerful, and yet so often tragically abortive American culture.

Scott Fitzgerald called his last collection of short stories *Taps at Reveille*. Bitter and brilliant, that title sums his life—and applies even more tellingly to Tom Heggen.

Tom, hail and farewell. Like Fitzgerald, a seemingly irrepressible, matinee-idoling, star-struck prodigy from the Middle West, you found no answer to the agony of your triumph, found only the black absence of an answer, and found that too soon, too young, too dead.

VI ❖ ❖ JOHN STEINBECK
A Lion in Winter

"A single best seller can ruin a writer forever."
>—JOHN STEINBECK'S REACTION TO THE 150,000
>HARD-COVER SALE OF *Of Mice and Men*
>(1937)

"It's so much darker when a light goes out than it would
have been if it had never shown."
>—FROM THE CLOSING CHAPTER OF HIS LAST
>NOVEL, *The Winter of Our Discontent*
>(1961)

"Remember him! Remember him!"
>—ELAINE STEINBECK, TO WELL-WISHERS IMME-
>DIATELY AFTER THE MEMORIAL SERVICE FOR
>HER HUSBAND (1968)

No OVERNIGHT VOLCANIC upthrust but a long ranging mountain was John Steinbeck. When I came to New York four years ago I picked up a newspaper and saw that my old friend John was in trouble.

Strike One—He was on his back in a hospital bed on the eve of an operation that sounded as if he was bucking Big C.

Strike Two—One of his sons had been arrested for possession of drugs. Actually it was marijuana, but from the size of the headlines one would have thought the lad had been caught with a million bucks of the heavy stuff: FAMOUS AUTHOR'S SON NABBED ON DOPE CHARGE!

Strike Three—? Well, Steinbeck was a big man, built for power and, despite years of literary fame and city living, still a raw-boned country boy from the ranch lands of Salinas, California. He was a ruddy outdoorsman, good at growing things, fixing engines, handling boats. He looked like a clean-up batter, a grizzled, bearded, sixty-year-old Duke Snider. Life had pitched him some pretty good curves, even his share of spitters, had tried to throw fast balls past him like a celestial Bob Gibson and hadn't been able to strike him out yet.

I called his wife, Elaine, who confirmed what kind of day he had had. Reporters hounding him for statements on his son's public embarrassment. John fuming and setting his bulldog jaw, harassed by searing pains of the body and of the spirit. The doctors had already begun to drug him against the crucial morning probe. She didn't know whether or not he would want me to see him in that condition. He was a physical man, furious at having to be in bed. He didn't mind if people saw him gloriously drunk once in a while, but he was as prideful about his physical well-being as he was about his loving care for language.

Still, she thought he might like to hear from me and gave me the room number.

A gruff, impatient voice on the other end of the phone said, "Yes? What do you want?" In that tone was a baseball bat waiting to swing at persistent reporters who would invade a man's most private moments to get their story.

I identified myself, said I had just come to town and—though it is always an empty question to ask a strong man who is made to lie down—wondered how he was feeling. "Rotten," Steinbeck said. "It's been one hell of a day. Where are you?"

I said I was about ten blocks away and didn't want to disturb him if—

"Hell, come on over."

Twenty minutes later I was walking into one of those depressingly antiseptic single rooms in an enormous, impersonal hospital on Manhattan's East River. There on his back lay the only living male Nobel Prize winner for literature. With his craggy mountain of a face, his powerful chest, his sturdy body, he looked too big for that hospital bed.

I said I had always enjoyed our talks. We had exchanged ideas, travel bits, book notes, gossip over friendly booze at Elia Kazan's parties, in the kitchen of his town house on Seventy-second Street, and other places over a bunch of years.

He grunted, closed his eyes in pain, cussed a little bit and snapped open and shut the blade of a large pocket knife.

"Don't know how much sense I'll make. The medics shoved a lot of pills into me. They're rolling me into surgery first thing in the morning."

He pointed a gnarled finger toward a white metal medicine cabinet. "You'll find some vodka in there. Make yourself a drink."

Glass in hand, I went back to the bedside. "I've brought you the book from the Watts Writers Workshop, John, *From the Ashes*. At the last class James Thomas Jackson and the other writers wanted to autograph it for you."

He picked it up and ran his hand over it. "A book. That's

great. I want to read it. When you see 'em thank 'em for me."

The book was no token gift to the most distinguished author in America. Steinbeck had been in direct contact with our Watts Workshop. When he saw *The Angry Voices of Watts* on national television he had taken time to send me a note:

> I was astonished at the quality of the material. Some of it was superb. For one thing I was impressed with the growth of these people. I am so tired of one-note writing, sad homosexuality is not enough as a working tool for a writer. Your writers have learned early that one is not aware enough to scream with pain if one has not had glimpses of ecstasy. And both belong in our craft—else there would be neither.

Our Workshop in Watts—called Douglass House in honor of the ex-slave Frederick Douglass, who became a powerful writer and orator in the abolitionist cause—originally had been supported by contributions from fellow-writers, Harry Golden, James Baldwin, Irving Stone, Paddy Chayevsky . . . Steinbeck's check arrived with a practical suggestion. Instead of my taking so much time writing to hundreds of individuals, apply to the National Foundation for the Arts. He was a member of its council and would put in a recommendation for us at the next meeting.

It had been John Steinbeck's characteristic combination of enthusiasm and practicality that had helped to make Douglass House more than just another fly-by-night creative venture in the ghettos.

Now, with pain and a dread of the unknown he faced in the morning interlacing his comments—at times punctuating them with disconcerting clicks of the knife he clenched in his hand—he spoke about the Watts phenomenon and black writing in general.

"I tell you something, I know they're angry and feel on the bottom, that they've got nothing because we took it all—but

I envy those young writers." To my surprise he reeled off the names of three or four from our Watts anthology. His memory, like his colleague John O'Hara's, always had been prodigious. "They don't have to search for material. They're living it every day. The subject matter is built-in dynamite. There's no luxury quite like having something to say."

He took a deep breath that expanded his chest against the straining sheet. "That's my trouble. I don't think I have anything to say any more. And yet, I'm like an old tailor. Put a needle and thread in my hand and a piece of cloth and I begin to sew. My hands have to keep busy. I have to hold a pencil in my fingers. I need to write some pages every day. When you do something for over thirty years, when you hardly think about anything else but how to put your experiences into the right words, you can't just turn it off and go out and play in the garden. I want to write every day, even if—I don't have anything to say."

Watching John Steinbeck lashing at himself in that frustrating hospital bed, I was reminded of the stag at bay, wounded possibly unto the death, but still flailing out with his antlers and refusing to go down.

"John, that's ridiculous. I don't see you often, but every time I do we talk for hours. I don't believe this crap about 'nothing to say.' "

"Go fix yourself another drink," he said. "You've got to drink for both of us. These damn pills." As I made my way to the makeshift bar, he asked, "How do you teach that class? I'd like to see it. I'd like to drop in. But I don't think I'll ever get to California again. Salinas is getting too big. Monterey—I hardly recognize it. I wonder if you feel that way about going back to Hollywood. Thomas Wolfe said it for all of us. 'You can't go home again.' I felt pretty low when I tried." He flipped the knife savagely. He always had been a strange amalgam of gentle and violent man.

"Damn it, got myself off the track. I was talking about your class. How do you teach 'em? What can you tell 'em about writing except putting things down honestly, precisely? 'I looked at the dog. The dog looked at me.' You can try fifty different ways, but you'll never be able to say it any better than that."

We talked about writing and what writers we admired and what writers we could live without. John was impatient with the Mandarin writing that is coming back into style, and with homosexual writing, impatient with excessive flourishes and deviation. In the thirties, with *In Dubious Battle* and the epic *Grapes of Wrath*, he had been a darling of the Communists and the social avant garde. Now he had become a curmudgeon to the Now Generation, who called him a warmonger for his stand on Vietnam and an old fogey for his attitude toward marijuana, acid, and speed. We disagreed about the war, but he was articulate on South Vietnam's side of it. He was hoping for peace, always had believed in peace, but there were times when man had to fight. As the Norwegians stood up to the Nazis in *The Moon Is Down*. I didn't think the two wars were analogous. I didn't say it, but I thought in this area John was living in the past.

We half-disagreed about the hippies. He was troubled by their indolence, their self-indulgence, their tendency to do more talking about art than actually to produce any. "This generation that thinks it's so hip could be the real Lost Generation," he said. "The proof will be in what they produce—and what kind of next generation they produce. We thought we had it bad in the thirties. But I've never seen a time when the country was so confused as to where it's headed. The trouble with the young people seems to be, they're trying to swing the wheel around and take off in some opposite direction. But no one was ever able to do that successfully without maps, without charting a course, taking readings, and knowing the next anchorage."

John Steinbeck was a good sailor, a good map reader, a dreamer with practical hands who knew how to moor his boat at Sag Harbor against the impending storm when neighbors were letting theirs swing and crash into each other. A mapless revolution, a chartless voyage offended the Yankee man of action in whom still beat the heart of a poet.

Tacking a little, while urging me to help myself at his white enameled bar, he compared the wandering hippies to the knights of the Middle Ages. John had made a lifelong study of Malory's *Morte d'Arthur*. With his usual thoroughness he had studied fifteenth-century English so he could read the Arthurian tales in their earliest translation. Fascinated by the material, he had planned a major work on the days of chivalry. And as always he had something of his own, uniquely original, to bring to what might have been either a romantic or an academic subject.

"You know in a lot of ways, Budd, those days are not so different from our own. An old order was on the way out. Something new was in the air, but no one knew exactly what lay ahead. The concept of chivalry was essentially a humanistic idea—going forth to do good deeds. Not just saving damsels in distress, but protecting the poor. It's no accident that Kennedy's Court was also called Camelot. But aside from the courtiers there were these individual knights roaming the land and searching for their own individual values. And there were the bad knights who only pretended to fight for the chivalric myth but were actually using the thing for their own selfish purposes. Maybe on the street corners today are our own Galahads and Mordreds. But it needed an Arthur, a Round Table, to hold them together and—"

"Hell, John, that could be a fascinating novel. In a strange way, a kind of *Grapes of Wrath* of the Middle Ages. I never thought of the period that way before!"

John worked his teeth together and stuck out his jaw defiantly. The pills were taking effect, and he was fighting them too. "I don't know . . . nothing to say . . . Did you see what the *Times* wrote about me . . . ?" On the medicine table near his bed was an editorial from the gray eminent *New York Times* wondering in print whether John Steinbeck deserved the Nobel Prize.

I tossed it back impatiently. "Who the hell are *they* to judge *you?* Could the pipsqueak who wrote that stupid paragraph ever write *Pastures of Heaven* or *Tortilla Flat, The Red Pony, The Long Valley, Cannery Row, East of Eden,* and now *Travels with Charley . . . ?*"

"Charley [his black poodle] helped me a lot on that one," Steinbeck grinned, and then grimaced. "And here's one from the *Post.*"

Another editorial, from the *New York Post,* was putting the great writer down for forsaking his old liberalism on Vietnam. The tone was snappish and unforgiving, as only a religiously liberal journal can lecture a prodigal son.

"John, if I were you I'd throw those lousy clippings away. It's like you're running your own anticlipping service. Only saving the put-downs. But they can't take the Pulitzer Prize away from you. Or the Nobel. Or *Grapes of Wrath.* Or two dozen books that make a monument. You'll be remembered in the twenty-first century, when nobody knows the name of the current put-down artist for the *Village Voice.*"

John Steinbeck made a kind of growling sound in his throat and flipped open his blade and made a gesture with it toward his belly. "I don't want to come out of this thing in the morning a goddamn invalid. When I'm not working on a book I've got to be outdoors, working on my boat, growing something, *making* something."

I looked at this big man imprisoned in this small, depressing room oppressed by nagging headlines and notices. It was no accident that his last novel had been entitled *The Winter of Our Discontent* and that the aging protagonist, significantly descended from sea captains but now subserviently tending a small grocery store, thinks to himself, "Men don't get knocked out, or I mean they can fight against big things. What kills them is erosion. They get nudged into failure."

It seemed incongruous for me to be searching for words to try and nudge a great man, and incidentally a marvelously warm human being, into a sense of his own glorious success.

A young Negro nurse appeared to administer some medicines. "You know it's after midnight," she said. "I wasn't supposed to let you stay so long, but you two were so busy talking together, and Mr. Steinbeck seemed to be enjoying himself—"

Maybe *The New York Times* no longer appreciated John Steinbeck, but clearly this young nurse dug him, not for who he was but what he was.

After midnight! I had been there five-and-a-half hours. And the man who had "nothing to say" had done most of the talking, on a score of provocative subjects. I only wish in this electronic age we both feared that I had been able to tape it for our literary history.

When I got to the main floor all the hospital doors were locked. I phoned my wife from the main reception desk to tell her I seemed to be locked in for the night. Finally a watchman let me out through a basement emergency door.

A few weeks ago I was on my way back to New York again. I told a mutual friend I would call Steinbeck as soon as I arrived. I had heard he was back in that hospital. While I was packing I turned on the TV news and learned that I was never going to see him again.

We arrived in New York the morning of the funeral. It was in a small Episcopalian church in midtown Manhattan. The ceremony took about twenty minutes. Henry Fonda, once the youthful star of the film version of *The Grapes of Wrath,* read a few favorite poems of John's and a relevant passage from *East of Eden.* The small church was half filled. There were a smattering of celebrities, John O'Hara, Frank Loesser, Richard Rodgers . . . Paddy Chayevsky said to me afterward, "I never knew him but I thought as a writer I should stop work for an hour and pay him homage."

But he seemed almost the only one. One might have thought every writer in New York would have turned out, and others from across the country. Of the out-of-towners, I recognized only Joe Bryan III, a gentleman writer from Virginia who is not ashamed of old-fashioned sentiment, not to mention old-fashioned virtues—like loyalty.

In the family room, Elaine Steinbeck embraced the score of friends who had shown up on this bleak Monday afternoon and said, "All I ask is, remember him. Remember him!"

"Remember him!" a European friend of mine said as we joined unconcerned passers-by on Madison Avenue outside the church. "Maybe I should not say this as I am a guest in your country, but if John Steinbeck had been one of ours there would have been a great procession down the Champs Elysées, all the members of the Academy would have marched, yes, and the young artists, too. Like when Camus died. The whole country went into mourning."

"Well, in our country we seem to reserve that kind of funeral for generals and motion-picture producers, and Cosa Nostra executives," I said. A few days earlier the Walter Wanger funeral had been SRO. But, of course, he had been married to Joan Bennett, had lived in a world of movie stars, had taken a potshot at his wife's lover, and had produced *Cleopatra*.

I had made my peace with Walter Wanger. And surely I would not begrudge him his funeral due. But it does seem incongruous that his passing should be marked with more pageantry and attendance than was granted to Steinbeck. But whether our farewell involved thousands of admirers, or merely the few hundred who were there, John Steinbeck was truly a lion in winter. Grizzled, wounded, but unbowed, he stormed forward even to what he feared was a losing battle in the final winter of his discontent.

Epilogue

I<small>N THE LIVES OF ALL</small> these eminently successful men, each of whom has suffered racking failures, there have been tragic, broken marriages, financial dislocations, and enough seemingly accidental and incidental woes to glut a Dickens or a Dostoevski. Each one rolled and bolted and staggered and shuddered with the punch in his own way. Would Fitzgerald's life have been less checkered if the wife he loved had not been doomed to sanitariums in their early thirties? Would Saroyan have been able to go on with the creatively happy-go-lucky time of his life if there had been peace-it's-wonderful instead of blitzkrieg and Auschwitz? Would Tom Heggen have gone on to become a mountain range instead of a fateful, solitary marker if he had conquered the disease of too much too fast . . . ?

. . . If, if, always the tragic, personal *ifs,* and yet I cannot escape the feeling—all right, the conviction—that from *Main Street* to *The Great Gatsby* to *The Grapes of Wrath* to *The Daring Young Man on the Flying Trapeze* to *Mister Roberts* runs a trembling connective line, like the significant scratchings of the seismograph signaling impact, earthquake, and danger. In each case, though in different degrees and chronological rhythms, sudden fame was followed by creeping failure. Either the real thing or its subjective shadow, a *sense* of failure.

In Scott Fitzgerald's personal library there are some volumes bearing a bookmark of his own device with a curiously apt drawing and inscription. It depicts a gay skeleton drinking a cocktail and the legend at the bottom says: "Be Your Age!" Scott's consistent, humorous double vision chose this odd *ex libris.* Could anything sum up more succinctly this haunting North American inability of our artists to grow up to themselves? Of my six friends, Red Lewis, Scott Fitzgerald, Bill Saroyan, Pep

West, Tom Heggen, and John Steinbeck, only Pep was spared the attrition of success. Wrapped proudly in his resounding "flop-eroos," he had learned to dig in and hang on against the cruel winds of failure. Of the high flyers who foundered in the doldrums, perhaps only Scott had begun to find the answer, but, to our dismay, found it too late, when he already had one foot in oblivion and the other in immortality.

Steinbeck, that sturdy yet hypersensitive Westerner, had one foot in immortality while feeling the other slipping into the quicksand of oblivion. The college kids, no longer into *The Grapes of Wrath,* were increasingly unaware of *In Dubious Battle* and the other good books that reached us thirty to forty years ago. Recently I mentioned Steinbeck to a well-educated young lady who recognized him only as the author of *Travels with Charley.* In search of his roots, his stubborn romance with the no longer good-old-U.S.A., he had gone back to the road, rediscovering America through the windshield of his camper. Young America had been on the road for at least a decade, searching for new values to replace the hypocrisy of puritanism, a heartless materialism, and our worn-out liberalism. Old John had gone forth like the Arthurian knights he admired, in the same quest, riding a Land-Rover instead of a mailed steed, brandishing a pen instead of a lance. Ironically, *Travels with Charley* wins a nod of recognition from the new generation at whose hands he had felt alienation and rejection.

Is Steinbeck to be once more rediscovered, by young readers, as Melville was rescued from oblivion forty years ago? Or will the likes of Leslie Fiedler (an honorable man with whom I happen to disagree) succeed in his undertaking of burying Steinbeck along with what he considers the wrongheaded practitioners of realism and naturalism?

As long as there is human exaggeration, myopia, hindsight, copycatting, and a constant shifting in the winds of fashion and opinion, writers will suffer, and succumb to or endure, their Seasons of Success. But just as we struggle to tame our hurricanes by dropping new chemicals into the eye of the storm, perhaps we as critics, as bookmongers, and as readers can begin to temper the fury of those Seasons:

So that a Nathanael West is allowed to earn his keep while practicing his art; so that a god hurled down from Olympus into the grubby marketplace is not forced to hack his stories at $250 a crack in order to stitch himself together for a desperate, final assault on the ramparts of self-fulfillment, and perhaps with it, immortality.

For a hundred years muscular U.S.A. has been the land of get-rich-quick, get-strong-quick, a nation that sung Herself in the vainglorious words of Walt Whitman, in the manifest destiny of Teddy Roosevelt, onward and upward, bigger and better, sweet land of General Motors, Ezra Pound, the Super Bowl, the Top Ten Songs, Actors, Writers, Football Teams . . .

Now an America troubled, an America chastened, an America no longer loved for its democratic potential or its ability to outproduce the world, prepares for its two-hundredth birthday with sigh and groan rather than with laughter and cheers. Perhaps we may find strength in our newly discovered weaknesses. Once we stop chorusing "I can do anything better than you can," or challenging "What have you done for me lately?"— perhaps we may begin to mellow, to mature, to find that there is a new world richer than any we know, beyond fame and fortune and the institutionalizing and the worship of fame and fortune that have clouded our vision, raised havoc with our artists, and driven some of the very best of them to failure in success.